God's Wild Man: Running Down the Truth

Scott Bartleson

Published by Scott Bartleson, 2021.

Table of Contents

God's Wild Man

Running Down the Truth

An autobiography of Scott Bartleson

Copyright © 2021 Scott Bartleson.

To my first and only love, Kelley.

Without her, I would be six feet under or, more likely, hundreds of body parts strewn across some embankment or highway.

For as many as are led by the Spirit of God, these are sons of God. (Romans 8:14)

Never Boring

Everything written here is from memory to the best of my recollection. This story is completely true, although some of the names have been changed to protect the innocent (or, in some cases, the guilty). Please excuse some of the language; it is not my intention to offend. I am just painting an accurate picture, much of which is ugly. The drunken scenes, early on in my story, are a close approximation of what happened, but I've left out some of the details as I was drunk at the time.

While writing this book, I recall what my father once told my new bride: "Your life will never be boring with this guy." Coming from a millionaire who mowed four acres of grass with a push mower next to a major road in his tighty whities, you would have thought a beautiful and intelligent girl like Kelley would have run. Over the years I have seen this time and time again. The beautiful and innocent girl thinks she can tame the lion. For poor Kelley, it was like trying to catch a train with a fishing pole. Good for me that she had a strong line. The poor girl was dragged down the tracks for years.

As for my writing, you'll have to forgive me as I didn't spend much time opening books in high school. They always came home with me but were rarely opened. As long as Mom saw me with the books, she thought all was well. In fact, I took my schooling so seriously that I was able to finish one of my final exams, multiple choice, in only a few minutes. The teacher handed out the answer sheets first before the actual questions were handed out. By the time he handed me the question sheet, I had already completed the exam. I was out the door, the class got a good laugh, and I was free. I've left you this example so you would overlook the crudeness of my writing from a deliberately uneducated man who happened to live a crazy but incredible life.

Chapter 1: Inner-City Youth

My grandfather lovingly called me "Piss and Vinegar." I was raised in the inner city, one of eight children, by a hardworking divorced mother, and my early life gave me plenty of things to be pissed about. My father visited infrequently, and, on one occasion, he told me that when I lost my temper, it destroyed brain cells. Nevertheless, I never seemed able to control that terrible temper.

Every one of us is gifted in some way, and, as a boy, I could read faces. From an early age, I could spot most liars a mile away. My divorced mother and her eight kids would sneak into a large Christian Reformed Church for Sunday morning service. We would usually sit in the balcony where there were less people. From this vantage point, I could observe all the people sitting below. It would have been preferable for the young "Piss and Vinegar" if the people who called themselves the "chosen of God" had treated their little kids better. Now, don't get me wrong, there were many nice, beautiful, loving people there. It's just that for a boy who's struggling and couldn't handle any more pain, the bad ones seemed to be wearing blinking neon clothes. Their bad behavior overshadowed their stuck-up faces.

The young mind is incredibly creative; it's just missing a lot of facts. One boy I knew—we called him Tarzan—said that his dad shot a bear right through the eye with his BB gun and killed him dead. This started me thinking that my BB gun could remove me permanently from this stuck-up Dutch worship community. If I could just sneak my BB gun into church and shoot the preacher, I wouldn't have to see all those noses in the air anymore. But I figured that Tarzan's dad had a better BB gun than I did, so I abandoned my plan, not from lack of will, but from lack of resources.

However, the BB gun did manage to get me in trouble. The neighbors out back started a Hatfield-and-McCoy kind of war with us. They bleached our garden, so I shot out their back windows with my BB gun. My mom made me apologize to Mrs. Hatfield. It went something like this: "I'm sorry . . . you old coot."

One of the Hatfield girls was Carol. Still seeking revenge, I convinced her that old rabbit crap was chocolate.

On the weekends, I'd schmooze the old ladies in the neighborhood, trying to earn some money for food and snacks. We had three meals a day, but the eight of us kids went through food like wolves. For a high-speed boy who was full of energy, it wasn't enough. With my mowing and raking money, I'd usually buy a half gallon of milk and a bunch of bananas. I was too young to know if the bananas were priced by the pound, piece, or bunch, so I'd just give the girl all my money and hope that I had enough. I would drink the milk straight down and hide the bananas under my pillow.

Occasionally, I had problems with bullies or black kids. One day, walking to school with my oldest sister, I found a much larger white kid beating up on one of my mouthy little black friends. I was probably in first or second grade at that time, and the bully was in fifth or sixth. I got ahold of the big kid's neck and pounded his face rather good. A couple of teenagers rewarded me with a handful of candy for bloodying up the bully. When I got inside the school building, I found my oldest sister before she went to class. I showed her my haul, and she stole most of it from me. Dog eat dog, and she sure was the female dog when I was growing up.

Some of the black kids in our neighborhood would have what they called "honky day." This was a day where the blacks would beat up the whites. I remember staying up late at night devising strategies and worrying how I would protect my sisters.

One summer day a large group of black kids jumped me. I must have been seven or eight at the time. They beat the crap out of me and stole my bike. They stripped most of the parts off it and left me with the frame. My anger over this one event cost me millions of brain cells, but I didn't care. I never wanted to suffer like that again, and I vowed that next time I'd win.

One of my friends had the misfortune of being beaten up by the black kids countless times. We would usually walk in groups so they wouldn't attack us, but he lived the farthest from school. He took regular beatings after everybody else peeled off from the group toward their homes. More than thirty years later, he's still brought to tears over the pain of these memories.

While you'll never see his story on television (or mine for that matter) in politically correct America, the truth is that blacks profiling whites for gang-style beatings happened quite frequently in the '70s, and I've heard that this is still happening in places today. One of my friends was severely beaten by four or five blacks swinging garden hoses cut into three- to four-foot lengths, with the brass end of the hose making dozens of nasty wounds.

By far, the worst gang I had to deal with was the Farrakhaners. These were black Muslim teenagers—part of the "peaceful religion." One evening, pedaling my bike at dusk, three Farrakhan teenagers shot me in the face at close range with pellet guns, hitting me three times. Luckily, they only had Crosman 760s, which didn't do any major or permanent damage.

Another time, I had to fight off these same three boys when they beat up my little brother while he tried to defend himself at the top of a large slide on the playground. I hurt one of the boys pretty bad, and they probably reasoned I was a crazy man when they took off. I was starting to get a reputation as someone not to be messed with. Some of the brothers called me Little Man because I fought like one. I mostly felt alone and had to rely on myself.

My dad had stopped spanking me because I told him it didn't hurt when it really did. This was just my way of saying that I didn't give a damn what he did. In truth, I was mad at him for leaving. My mom had an incredible work ethic and managed to keep the house together. She did a wonderful job with the tools she had available, but we gave her a lot of trouble, most of which came from me, and which, looking back, I wish I could undo. By the time I was nine or ten, I had lost all respect for authority. I burned the bushes on the church property just for a kick; it was one way for me to poke at the stuck-up folks there.

Somehow, I got ahold of some *Outdoor Life* magazines. For an inner-city kid, the bear stories and wild places made me dream of living in a trapper's cabin all by myself—just me and my pet grizzly. There was something about a big old moose with huge antlers, living in the woods, and me eating moose steaks for dinner. This became my life's dream.

One of our neighbors, who I'll always remember fondly, was an old guy named Pete. He was a mechanic and an inventor and went to the same church we attended. He was a righteous, humble old man. This saint always fixed our bikes, and he did more for our family than anyone I can remember.

One time he told me about some rich guy who offered to buy his house for more than it was worth. The guy wanted him to live there for free because he needed the tax write-off. It sounded like this fellow was just trying to bless him. But it didn't pass the smell test, so Pete would have no part of it. In his simple middle-class world, it made no sense to deliberately lose money, and his upbringing told him not to do anything that even appeared evil.

My mother taught first grade, so she had the summers off. As her finances stabilized, she was able to take us out camping for two weeks. I don't know how she managed her wild crew without pulling her hair out, but she took us all over the West and planted a good seed in my heart that would later grow.

My two best friends were Rob and Mark. Rob was a tall, lanky white kid, and man was he funny. Mark was a stout black kid who was super slick and an accomplished shoplifter. I used to follow him into the store, but I could never catch him in the act. We'd get outside the store, and he'd give me a Snickers bar, my favorite, when he hadn't bought a thing.

One time, Mark and I were walking down the street a few blocks from school. One of the guys from the "honky day" crowd let his Doberman Pinscher loose on us and called Mark an Uncle Tom. I kicked the dog as hard as I could, right in the throat. That stopped him, and Mark gave the dog's owner a beating. Just one more peaceful day in the city.

We played tons of basketball, and we played rough. We called one of our friends "Basketball Booty" because he looked like he had a basketball in the back of his pants. Mark's and Basketball Booty's parents gave them a "Christian" education, which I'm sure they thought would get them out of the hood. Mark spent decades in jail, and Basketball Booty is serving a life sentence for a murder he committed at nineteen while robbing someone's house.

There were two kids in our school who ranked high in the stuck-up crowd. They loved to pick on one kid who was really fat. His last name started with an O, and these two used to call him Big O, which was just an underhanded way of calling him fat. One day, when everything seemed to be going wrong, I just started pounding on these two, telling them that this was the end of the Big O bullshit. Later that summer, I built the fat kid a nice skateboard. I had a sense of sympathy for the underdog, not realizing that I would probably be considered one too.

In fourth or fifth grade, I had this old teacher. Her face was harsh and wrinkled, and she looked like she survived by just chewing her nails. Since I could read faces, I knew from the get-go that I was not her favorite student. She was intent on performing a play for a special event, and she took it very seriously. The plot was some "Ozzie and Harriet" type family fairytale that had no resemblance to mine. The whole storyline somehow made me feel dirty because I was one of the few kids in school that didn't have a dad at home.

She put me in the front row of the choir. Now, the front row is usually a good place to put a kid if you want to keep your eye on him, but with this kid it didn't work out so well. I hatched a conspiracy with Rob, the baker's son, and Brett that none of us would sing. As the play started, the crew held their mouths shut, but, as the play progressed, I started to lose my muted friends as, one by one, they began to sing. This was my first lesson on people caving in to peer pressure and doing what authority expected.

I was made of sterner stuff, and I did my best to ignore the glares of the stuck-up Dutch and the tears of my mom. I never sang a word. I felt like my friends had been castrated by the crowd, but after this I was more popular than ever, and everyone was put on notice that this boy would not bend unless he broke. And break I would, much later in life.

I managed to make it to the sixth grade where I had run-ins with two adopted kids. The one fellow was a school safety—the kind with an orange vest and a steel bar that stops traffic for the kids. He was harassing my sisters one day when I decided that I'd had enough. He was older and bigger than me, but I surprised him by getting the staff away from him and beating him with it.

The other kid had a worse temper than I did; he'd punch you at the drop of a hat. The two of us got into an all-out brawl. We were trading punches when two teachers ran up. One grabbed my right arm while the other grabbed my left. The kid just continued punching me in the face until a third teacher arrived. Teachers have ways of exacting their revenge.

I found myself popular, but not really needing it. I saw how everybody seemed to compromise what they believed just to get along. This made me want to be alone more and more. Every school has its calendar of events, and mine had some kind of party scheduled, but I couldn't have cared less. My mom and busybody sisters felt there was something wrong with me because I really didn't want to go. All the kids were dressing up as fairy-tale or cartoon characters, and they were going to have snacks and games in the gym.

I remember one of my dad's business associates commenting on how he had never seen me smile, and I think this bothered my parents and sisters. I agreed to go to the party as long as I got to choose the character and the outfit. I decided on the emperor with no clothes, so I went to the party in my long underwear. I still can't believe Mom let me go. Running around at night in my drawers had finally paid off. Deep down inside, I was still giving the bird to the stuck-up Dutch. I had a great time. Although I only got second place in the costume contest, most of my friends said I got robbed.

I ended the school year thinking that at least I had two good friends who were almost as careless and cynical as I was. These two would stand with me, this I knew.

Then we moved.

Chapter 2: Country Life

The next year, we left the city. My dad started making big money and bought my mom two lots on the Thornapple River. It was good for me to get out of the city. We had an abandoned twenty acres next to us along the river. I shot my first rabbit with a pellet gun. He died slowly, and I cried—some kind of mountain man.

I worked for a lawn service and had my own money. I bought a shotgun and a .22 caliber rifle to hunt pheasants and rabbits. I also got a twelve-foot powerboat. Cruising up and down the river full blast, I knew where all the rocks were.

I was probably fourteen when I bought a .44 caliber 1860 black powder pistol. I don't remember my mom giving me any grief about my guns—what a wonderful woman. When my Uncle Abe found out I had a pistol, he chastised my mom for giving me just enough rope to hang myself.

Mom sent us to Dutton Christian School. The teachers there seemed to be more competent and honorable than the city school staff. I respected most of them, but there's always one who rubs you the wrong way. Little did he realize that he was battling with an eighth-grade-delinquent tactical genius. Because I only had one teacher to deal with, I could spend all my energies on him—and basketball, of course. I was determined that this would be his last year of teaching there. The boys and I saw to it.

I'll change the teacher's name just to protect his identity and reputation. The first day of class, Jack told us how he had just returned from the mission field, and the children oohed and aahed and called him "Sir," practically licking his boots. I had a slick way of swearing in class. I would turn my head to the side, faking a snotty-load cough, and I'd cough out a word like "bullshit." It's difficult to describe the sound—basically it was sixty percent cough and forty percent "bullshit." The class loved it, but Jack was not pleased.

The war had begun.

Jack had a poster of Albert Einstein, who he worshiped. After all, it was a science class. I put a big glob of green Jell-O right under Albert's left nostril. Jack also had some prized fish in an aquarium. Phenol red and other assorted chemicals took care of them. The lab was quite nice for a private school. There was a large ventilation system that Jack was proud of. Sometimes we would start alcohol fires on the stone benches just to get him to turn on this system. One day at break, I climbed onto the roof and stuffed the ventilation system full of rocks. We started a nice fire, and he came to the rescue and turned on the fans. The ventilation system sounded like a fifty-car pileup.

We never gave Jack a break. I put an alcohol burner under the seat of one of the chairs. It turned the metal orange hot. The burner was put back. The steel was no longer orange, but it was still hot. A girl took her seat for class and burned her pants good.

Because Jack had to deal with the possibility of fires in his lab, he had systems in place. He put coffee cans with sand near each stone table. I planted beans in them and watered the seeds regularly. Once the beans had sufficiently grown, we started another fire. Jack tried to save the day. Off came the lid of the coffee can to squelch the fire with the sand smothering system. But as hard as he tried, he couldn't get sand to come out. He now had a potted bean plant. Of course, we had a fire extinguisher in the hall. I saved the day, spraying some of my classmates in the process.

One day Jack found me imitating him in the hall with some friends. This poor guy was starting to come unhinged. He had had enough. He started pounding on me. He knew I was the primary instigator, but he couldn't prove it. This had gone too far, but we were relentless. The worst was yet to come.

One of the boys got hold of a twenty-inch rubber band used in commercial packaging and we found a way of stringing it across the back of the lab. We would wrap a piece of lead, a little smaller than a stick of gum, pull the rubber band back, release the lead with incredible speed and accuracy, and have the whole apparatus hidden in less than five seconds.

If there were enough kids present, the pulling of the rubber band could be done undetected. I don't remember who did it, but Jack got hit in the face. It stunned him and left a mark. We were lucky he didn't lose an eye.

A few weeks later he hit one of my friends, who had a broken leg and a big mouth, over the head with his own crutches.

This was the beginning of the end for poor Jack. He really wasn't that bad of a guy, he just destroyed himself with his arrogant boasting at the beginning of the school year. This wasn't a mission or military school, and he really blew it. I learned a lot from this. Sometimes, if you get off to a poor start with someone, it may be better just to pack it in. First impressions and all that.

It really was horrible what we did to Jack. I acknowledge now that I was the instigator of a mob. Our pranks had crossed the line. We had become predators. These kids all came from Christian homes, but where were the Christian hearts? I was just as bad now as the Dutch kids were back in the inner city. I saw myself as so much better than Jack that I'd allowed myself to become even worse.

I had learned to play basketball in the ghetto, and my excessive, abundant energy was focused on the game while at Dutton Christian. I'd practice basketball with my brothers for hours each day, and the kids I played basketball with honed me to a star player.

During the playoffs, I stole the basketball and scored the winning point that got us into the state finals. A few days later, however, I broke my hand punching a guy in the face who was beating up one of my friends. I couldn't play basketball, and we lost the state championship. The coach said I was his best player. We lost because of my temper. My coach cried, and it made me sick to let him and the team down.

I needed people after all.

Chapter 3: Back to the City

For some reason, my mom bought a house in the city, and we were back to the city schools. Although she tried to sell her house in the country, she wasn't able to. Looking back on it, the city is nowhere to raise kids. There are just too many bad influences, and it's easy to find trouble. Up until this point, I hadn't tried alcohol or drugs. This would change, and it brought with it the seeds of disaster that just about killed me on numerous occasions. The one thing I learned at Dutton Christian was the slicker you were, the longer you were in the game. Before that, I hadn't cared if I got caught. Now it had become a serious hobby not to be caught. I had matured as a delinquent and was hot after girls.

I played drums in the school band and normally spoke very respectfully to the band director, but I gambled and caused general mayhem on the sly. Because I had good manners, he thought the other two drummers were a bad influence on me. But I was the one who started just about everything, and it was hilarious. We were constantly doing harmless pranks. It was great fun.

There was a kid in our class with a big head. I called him Honeycomb after the cereal commercial, "Honeycomb's big, yah yah yah, it's not small, no no no." I was at the top of the food chain now and a first-class asshole some of the time.

One time, I saw one of the large male teachers verbally and physically abusing some little black kid. My "justice meter" went to the red. This guy deserved the thrashing we gave Jack and then some. Rob and I gave that teacher as much grief as possible.

There was a huge double standard that I didn't see at the time. It was somehow okay for me to tease Honeycomb, but this teacher was like a guard in the gulag to me. My sense of justice had become selfish and twisted. What had happened to that boy who was making skateboards for fat kids? It would be many years before he would show up again.

This teacher tried to get me expelled because I told him I didn't believe in God, and he caught me carving something in the woodwork while in a state of boredom. The board let me stay in school mostly out of respect for my mom. I dated three different beauties and then was off to high school for more of the same, but with tons of alcohol and fast cars—a bad combo.

Chapter 4: The Craziness Begins

I started drinking in high school. We had a friend who worked at a party store. We'd give him cash, and he'd set the booze behind the dumpster. There was another party store that never carded anyone, but it was in one of the worst neighborhoods—the kind of place you see in movies. You would hold your breath while you bought your booze, wishing you had eyes in the back of your head so you could dodge that empty whiskey bottle chucked by the big homeless guy that you had to pass when you left. You would get your booze, take a breath, and walk out like you owned the place with your four bottles of Mad Dog 20/20. Then you would drive like madmen and howl at the moon.

By this time, there were few people who would get in my car if I was driving. Pat was one of my friends whose dad warned him, "I really love Scott, but he's going to get you killed." I used to tell people that I never had an accident; they were always on purpose. When you drive 120 mph with your lights off, that's the truth.

Rob and I had the most balls, or the least brains, depending on how you looked at it. We used to get drunk and see how close we could get to sideswiping pimp cars. Occasionally we made contact, and then we would have pimps in hot pursuit.

We would shoot three-inch bottle rockets out of the backseat windows all over the inner city. One time, Rob, Warren, and

Chris got caught by nine cops. These officers couldn't believe that these white dudes were shooting it up in the hood with bottle rockets. We were all lucky that we didn't get shot.

After spending a night out drinking, I dropped Rob off in front of his house and drove away. He took a few steps and passed out in his front yard. About nine o'clock in the morning, a buddy of ours, who we called Jesus John, saw what looked like a dead man in Rob's front yard. Two little black kids were poking him with sticks to see if he was alive. Not to worry, it was just Rob sleeping off a drunken binge.

Another time, I dropped Rob off, and he went into the wrong house. When the owner of the home awoke in the morning, he was horrified to find Rob on his couch. When he woke up, Rob asked, "Who decorated this place?"

One of us stole a nice high-pressure fire extinguisher and we would spray pedestrians and cars. One time, we drove up to two stuck-up Ken-and-Barbie types walking in a high rent area. Ken gave me a snide, preppy look as we approached a stop sign and said, "Aren't you guys cool?" Ken and Barbie got the whole fire extinguisher.

They thought that by running in the grass, closer to the houses, they could get away from us, but poor Ken underestimated my driving skills. Curbs, lawns, bushes, and small trees couldn't stop me when justice needed to be served. Ken got the taste of justice probably for the first time—400 cubic inches of Pontiac power with a wild man at the wheel.

Another time, I hosed down the worker at a hamburger drive-through. Minutes later, as we were driving off from spraying the taco joint drive-through, we saw the cops arrive at the hamburger place one hundred yards or so down the street. They couldn't catch that old Pontiac.

I used to be able to imitate black people's voices quite well, so I'd go to the drive-through, order the food, and start this fake fight between a black man and his lady. I'd shout things like "Shut up, Walona." I'd slap my hands and curse, so it sounded like the black couple was having an all-out brawl at the drive-through voice box.

The person taking the order couldn't see the car or the people until they pulled up for the food. As two white guys driving up to pick up our order with straight faces, it was hilarious to see most of the crew inside gawking, expecting to see a bloody and beat-up black couple.

Number three of the three musketeers was Warren, otherwise known as Goof. Goof was a lovable, gullible addict. He smoked dope like it was oxygen, and one day the cops busted him. He had scored a large bag of weed, and he was so thrilled that he was throwing it up in the air as he skipped down a main street. He didn't even notice the officers driving by. Goof must have thought that slick just meant slippery.

But man could he drive. We did some incredible street chases. He mastered the powerslide where he could change directions with the emergency brake and still stay in his lane. He'd practice throwing knives for hours and could stick a tree at thirty feet. Goof ended up being a DJ and an accomplished Elvis impersonator. He could really sing.

We were tight for years, but one day Goof decided he was moving up. He was going to a burger joint, not with his two best buds, Rob and me, but with a carload of preppies. After arguing with us, Goof agreed that Rob and I could ride in the trunk. Rob was horrified. As we approached the busiest street in town—28th Street—Rob sought justice.

First the car jack was thrown out. Then, assorted items flew away. Finally, out went the spare tire. It was unbelievable how long that tire weaved through traffic. We found the trunk much roomier now. A few months later, Goof asked us a rather curious question. "Hey dudes, who would steal a spare tire? I got stranded last night."

"How would we know? Were you with your preppy friends? You know how those preppies are, sons of thieves, politicians, and preachers."

I came out of the gym one day, and three preppy jocks had my cousin surrounded and were busting his chops. These boys were all clean-cut climbers, always climbing over someone else to get to the top. I let them know if they ever touched my cousin again, I'd kick the crap out of all of them.

My uncle told me years later, with tears in his eyes, that I had helped my cousin more than I knew. My cousin was big and strong and with a little training he could have pounded them, but he was a teddy bear. He's the only kid I knew that actually read his Bible in this huge Christian high school.

I assumed that most of the high school teachers were schmucks and losers. Two of them were fooling around with the girls, who were vulnerable, and I had caught several other teachers in lies. The sociology teacher spent his time making smart remarks to the boys in class, trying to humiliate his competition for teenage girls. Just another phony playing like he was a Christian so he could pay his rent and fill his bed. The whole system stunk, and I couldn't wait to get out of there.

I found square dancing in gym class boring. However, if one was to change the record speed from 33 rpm to 45, then, when you spun your partner round and round, you could get some of the lighter girls to catch air.

Another time, my biology teacher said, "These stuffed squirrels are not flying squirrels" after my creative use of the displayed animals.

I was in a particularly devilish mood the day that I was set free from the stuck-up Christian Reformed school. We were waiting outside a locked door for class. How was I supposed to know the teacher was setting up for the exam in the room when I karate kicked the door?

"All right, Scott, we've had enough of your antics. You don't really want to be here, do you?"

"Huh, how'd you guess, sir?"

"Scott, I don't want you coming back. Why don't you tell your mother you want to go to another school?"

I'm thinking, *I'll lie for you mister, anything to get out of this pathetic place, staffed with liars and halfwits. All I could learn there was how to be a climber like the Ken and Barbie types at the school. You can have your little stuck-up world. I'll make my own way, sir. Thank you.*

Chapter 5: Country Crazy

My Christian school counselor had never spoken with me, but he told my mother that he had. I had a low GPA, and he said I could never get into college with that. I told him I didn't need college because I had plenty of money since I worked all the time.

My last two years of high school were at public schools back out in the country, and it was a breath of fresh air. My counselor was actually helpful. He made it possible for me to get into college. He was astounded that I had no idea what was required.

I was halfway through my junior year, but no one had ever explained the importance of college. Knowing this, my GPA went straight up. Thanks to Mr. Wasoric doing his job, I eventually ended up going to Michigan State University.

I don't remember the reason, but later in my junior year I moved in with my dad. He had dirt bikes, snowmobiles, and fourteen acres to run them on. I set up an Evel Knievel dirt jump. I was able to catch some incredible air with that 250 Yamaha. One day, I lost control. I had pushed the bike too fast for that jump, and I crashed into the barn, destroying both the bike and my back.

Dad used to take us to Drummond Island where he had a cabin. They got lots of snow up there. Dad told my brother and me to run the road once before we opened the snowmobiles up, to go all out. But Bobby was sticking to my sled like glue. I got tired of him riding my tail and went full throttle. Hitting a six-foot snowdrift at 100 mph, I ended up a hundred and forty paces from the snowdrift, having slid on my belly. I was lucky to be alive.

Having been through so many close calls, I started to feel indestructible. I had professional boxing gear. Friends would bring over the local tough guys, and none of them could match my punching power. I was 185 pounds and could carry two railroad ties on my shoulders for 150 feet. I could punch through a bag of concrete like it was white bread.

My best country bud was Boyd. He was a skinny kid with glasses, but good company. We used to fish and hunt together, and we shared a locker at school. There were three or four bullies at the country school. A couple of brothers were particularly bad.

Boyd never told me that they had been picking on him for some time. One of the brothers came up to me with his two big black friends and asked me if Boyd and I were queers. I told him that if he opened his mouth again, I'd knock his jaw clean off his face. His black buddies said that their brother was bigger than they were, and they'd go get him to finish me good. I told them to go get the whole f-ing tribe, and I'd beat their black asses all the way back to Africa.

You can take your politically correct fingers out of your ears now; this was, in fact, acceptable back in the hood. I first heard ghetto smack like this coming from my black buddy Mark. The brothers used the n-word back then much more than the whites ever did. I'm not saying I'm proud of the way I talked, I'm just telling you the truth. When I set out to share my story, I decided to tell it warts and all. I'm never running for political office, so I speak the truth, and I'm sorry if it offends you.

Anyway, the backwoods brothers just got their first dose of ghetto smack. A few weeks later, Loudmouth found out my word was good.

I was late for class, and Loudmouth, who sat behind me, insulted me as I walked in. I hit him so hard that I thought I broke his neck. He moaned and gurgled behind me while I calmly sat down. Under my breath, I said, "If I didn't break your jaw, I'll finish it later."

The little-old-lady teacher, who had probably watched him bully other kids for years, said in a sweet voice, "He probably deserved that." There was a different standard here, clean-cut climbers weren't protected.

Next, they sent Pat after me. He couldn't breathe normally for five minutes after just one punch. Later, we became good friends. One of the last guys dumped hot soup on my head in the cafeteria. I hit him twice, breaking all his ribs on one side. The shop teacher shouted at me, and it's good he did. His voice broke my concentration and slowed my momentum. I had so much punching power, and I was rolling full out with tunnel vision in a rage. One of those punches to the throat or head could have killed that kid. The word was out that "the city kid has dynamite in those hands." It was smooth sailing from then on.

There was a kid in our shop class who was the school narc. One day, we had a student teacher, and I figured I could get away with giving this kid a good bashing. When she wasn't looking, I took to clobbering this farm boy. She sent me to detention, which we called the "rubber room." Mr. Gillespy, a weightlifter, ran the "rubber room." I used to announce, "Hi, Mr. Gillesbian!" as I walked in. The fellow detainees would cheer. This time, Mr. Gillespy quickly told me to leave.

The student teacher was visibly shaken that I had been kicked out of the "rubber room," so she sent me to the office. When I reached the office, it was empty. There was nothing left for me to do but return to class and tell her that I had been kicked out of the office. The poor woman was flustered and told me that she didn't care where I went. "You mean I can go fishing? Thanks!" Spraying the class with a fire extinguisher was the icing on my delinquent mind's cake.

Country crazy is a whole lot different from city crazy. Instead of bottle rockets, it was .22 rifles in the back seat, shooting rabbits at night in the ditches, sneaking onto people's property to shoot deer, driving your car on ice-covered lakes at one o'clock in the morning as fast as you could on the highway, and drinking hundreds of gallons of beer.

Now educated in two different worlds, I somehow always gravitated to the wildest crowd. My wife says *I* was the wildest crowd. It was starting to get crazy, and people were going to start dying. Raising hell is like an addiction. Every weekend, it seems that you need more, and the more reckless, the more fun.

Unfortunately, before I left MSU, one of my city buddies and one of my country buddies would be dead.

Chapter 6: Three Brushes with Death

I had outrun a couple of cops with my DT360, which was an adrenaline pumper if there ever was one, and when I was drinking, it made for double trouble. The old Pontiac ran around 140 mph, top speed. The previous owner had put some high-performance parts under the hood, and I could outrun Trans Ams. Even stock cars couldn't do that. I was skilled at losing the cops.

I'd usually outrun the cops at night. I'd be running between 80 and 100, and I would see the bubble flashing. I'd shut my headlights off. If I kept my speed up and didn't touch the brakes, my car would virtually disappear. As soon as my lights were out, I'd run it up to about 120 mph in the dark. I pulled that stunt over twenty times and never got caught. A Kentwood cop told one of my friends that they got my license number thirteen times but could never catch me behind the wheel. That didn't make much sense to me at the time. I didn't think the cops had gotten that close.

One time, my buddy Dale and I were drunk when we decided to head out to Duncan Lake to run the ice with his old hot rod Chevy. Dale, in his drunken state, took a shortcut to the lake. As we sped between two lakefront houses, blissfully unaware of the large retaining wall between the house and the lake, we caught some serious air, looking like a *Dukes of Hazzard* action scene. Somehow, we made it to the lake with no major repairs or police involvement.

One of my older buddies was a forty-year-old hippie named Sonny. He was the local pothead who lived a few miles down the road. He was a piece of work, yet in many ways a good, honest man. He understood too well that the justice system had little to do with real justice.

One of my favorite stories about Sonny was how he got his Christmas tree one winter. He had been doing work around a rich man's house, and the guy refused to pay. Sonny wasn't going to small claims court. He just backed his old C10 pickup truck into the man's front yard and cut off the top of a beautiful spruce with his chainsaw. He brought the top home and decorated it for Christmas. I always admired him for taking the law into his own hands—a wonderfully funny, pothead patriot.

I'd run to the city when the country bored me. I could catch up with my city friends, or I'd find trouble without them. One time, I crashed a huge party. I was the only white person there and didn't know anyone. So I danced with some pretty black girls and had a great time. I told the DJ that the music sucked and gave him my Rolling Stones tape. They liked it, even "Brown Sugar."

One of my other friends wrapped his car around a tree. He persisted in a brain-dead state for years. My little brother hit a tree at high speed in my dad's Turbo Mercedes. The police officers at the scene of the accident told him that if it hadn't been a Mercedes, he and his girlfriend would have been dead.

I believe he was following my lead; he was outrunning a cop at the time.

It seems like the next three events were some long dream where you think you're drowning but can't wake yourself up. How could anyone be as reckless and stupid as I was? Really, what was the point? Even now, over thirty years later, I feel like yelling, "What the hell were you thinking?" To this day, I can't totally answer that, but for me at least there was a happy ending. When you are in the deep state of rebellion that I was in, the craziness must end. There are only two ways out—either death or sanity.

There was a cement plant right next to the East Beltline, and a local cop was laid up there, waiting for me to come back from Grand Rapids. I'd outrun him many times, but tonight they had given him a faster car. He was on me tight, and turning off the lights wasn't enough. That old Pontiac was pushing 140 with the lights off. My dad's street, Kraft, was my ace in the hole. It peeled off the beltline at about a fifteen-degree angle. If you didn't touch the brakes, the cops couldn't see you turn. I had this turn down to a science. If I was running 120 mph, I would let off the gas at 68th Street. By the time I coasted to Kraft, I had slowed down enough to make the turn without hitting the guardrail.

The problem this night was that I was drunk and running full out when I let off the gas at 68th Street. I hit the turn 20 mph too fast and six beers too many. I wiped out the driver's side of the old Pontiac but somehow made it home without the flashing bubbles catching me. The passenger side of my Pontiac was perfectly pristine, without a scratch. The driver's side was about demolished. I used to tell my dates they were perfectly safe with me as I always took the impact on my side.

I made the last Kraft run with Goof's mom's Toyota. I was about a year out of college, and I was explaining to him that *slick* had two meanings. Goof's teeth were chattering loudly, irritating me, and I cussed at him to stop it, all the while seething, "How the hell do you turn off the lights?" I could only get the wipers flying full speed. Somehow, we figured it out, and Goof got to live through my crazy reality for one night.

On the same weekend as the drunken getaway with the racecar cop, Boyd was abusing my Pontiac. I was out shooting my 12 gauge, and Boyd was out in my dad's field tearing it up with my car, just trashing my Pontiac. I yelled at him to stop, but he either didn't hear me or didn't want to. After he sped past me in the field, I shot my own car twice. He got the point, and hey, now my driver's side looked even more cool. I found out later that Boyd went to school telling everybody that we got in a gang fight in the inner city, and that was how my car got shot up.

A few months later, Boyd and I were at a party at Green Lake. My alternator was going bad, so my lights would fade in and out. One of my headlights was loose and swung back and forth from the guardrail incident. We picked up two girls, but they soon regretted it. I steered the car off the main road at a high speed, making an incredible power slide onto Green Lake Road.

One of the girls was screaming, her long nails digging into my neck. As we made the turn and slid through the stop sign, a state cop rolled up behind us. All the while I was just cracking jokes, and one of the girls said she had to pee.

The cop asked who I was trying to impress. I explained to him that the alternator was bad, and that if you didn't keep the gas near full throttle, the lights would fade out. Well, there was *some* truth in that statement.

He frowned. "Son, have you been drinking?"

"Yes sir, I had a couple of beers."

"How old are you, son?"

"Sir, I'm eighteen, but I look like I'm twenty-one, sir."

"Will you please walk along the white line for me now?" And then: "Please say your ABCs."

"A B C D E F G H I J K L M I C K E Y, Mickey Mouse." At this point my partners in crime were laughing, almost in tears. I think Blondie peed herself.

To this, the smiling cop dismissed us with, "Son, listen, you need to get them lights fixed. Have a good evening."

The smart thing to do would be to just slowly cruise out of there. But I was out to make history, plus I had told him that the car would only go fast. I was stretching the truth a bit though. I must have left a 30-foot patch as I fled the scene with

Mr. State Boy, bubbles on, in hot pursuit. I got her up close to 80 and just shut my lights off a few minutes or so later.

Boyd says, "Hey bud, isn't this the road with that huge iron pipe right in the middle?" I flashed the lights on, and we just missed that chunk of steel by inches. The girls were screaming regularly now. I made a sharp turn off onto some farmer's field with a real high hill that we could hide the car behind. We never saw that cop again, or the girls for that matter.

I stayed home from school one day, fishing or riding my 360. I don't remember which. I just decided I'd skip school that day. Pat came screaming down the drive. "Hey man, you sure picked the right day to skip! The new kid showed up with a 12 gauge to your first hour class looking for you!"

Before this, the new kid had beaten up a small hemophiliac kid in woodworking class. My justice meter went off. I told him that the next time he was feeling big and bad to look me up. The kid was about my size, and he just said he'd shoot me. I just laughed it off and, when I'd see him, I'd fashion a fake gun pose and go "bang-bang," mocking off a shot.

Come to find out, the new kid had just come from an institution that he had been in for quite some time. His dad had come home from Vietnam and shot his family, all except him, and they were trying to get this kid back into society.

Today, I still think about the scars that the war left on him so many years later. I bet he's locked up today, or he killed himself. How's a kid supposed to cut through that much crap and somehow be normal?

I'd had three brushes with death in a row, so what's the logical thing to do?

Chapter 7: Slowing Down the Crazy Train

Boyd wanted the Pontiac. For my part, I thought that a Chevy with a 350-rocket engine might be faster, and I was sure the Honda bike was. Logic is for the book types, but freedom is for cowboys—and patriots. They don't argue with you while you and your friends sit around like a bunch of Tories in togas, just talking.

But a cowboy just goes out and grabs it. After all, it wasn't logic that gave us an America that used to be free. The founders of America fought the biggest and best army in the world when they didn't even have a good supply of powder. Logic would have said, "Be a Tory." No, I had left those Tories two years ago. I was going to climb the biggest hill to see what was on the other side. Until this boy found his place, it was high speed, my way, get out of the way.

I was having a conversation with my grandpa about my dad leaving us in the ghetto. I told him that sometimes I felt like beating my dad for leaving us alone. My grandfather laughed at me. He said, "You're just full of piss and vinegar, boy. Don't you realize your dad worked twenty hours a day, seven days a week for seven years straight? He fought the good fight, but all that money don't really mean nothing, son. He paid too heavy a price."

I didn't know it at the time, but Dad had believed a lie, and so did I. Dad had paid a heavy price for those millions he made. They cost him his family. He became so wealthy he didn't know who he could trust. This would eventually come to destroy his fortune and his last days.

People have been debating how much behavior is related to genetics and how much of it is environmental. When I was a kid, I hardly knew my dad, and I'm running around the ghetto in my underwear. Dad's mowing his yard in the same. It must be genetics.

What had become of me? I'd become an addict of sorts. Why couldn't I just let off steam at the gym? Why couldn't I just have an evening of bowling or cards? What's wrong with normal? Why couldn't I just back off the pedal? When it comes to danger or drunkenness, and usually both, an addict always needs a little more speed or a little more beer.

I used to be a supreme prankster, but, before the ride ended, I was going to be gangster. What was wrong with me? What was feeding my head? If I didn't stop soon, Kelley said that I was going to wind up dead. She was my girl now—and man, what a beauty.

We met at Pat's graduation party. She was a beautiful blonde. One of my buddies drove her home with me in tow. By the second date, I told her that I was going to marry her. Her lack of understanding about what was going on around her made her somehow pure, divine, like a butterfly that has yet to fly. Her pureness and beautiful heart would keep me out of the grave, and she would eventually give me eight high-speed children. I made the best decision of my life, though I didn't realize it yet. For her, it was probably her worst.

I paid for college out of my own pocket. I worked seven days a week in the summers. They placed me on the eleventh floor in Hubbard Hall at Michigan State University. They couldn't have put together a wilder bunch of guys if they had planned it. I shared a room with a guy whose dad was in federal prison. He was a funny little Italian, and we got along pretty well.

By this point, the drinking was really starting to control me. It wasn't that I had to drink. It was just that when I started drinking, I felt powerless to stop. I started losing track of time. I was drinking so heavily that I would have blackouts, some of them for extended periods. A few of these times, I got in fights, and I didn't remember a thing.

While drunk one night, we filled a keg full of water and threw it out the window from the eleventh floor. It hit the cement right in front of some guy leaving the building, breaking the concrete sidewalk.

Another time three Notre Dame football players were trashing the dorm, and I got into a scrap with all three. I broke a window out, and one of the players, with some help from me, almost went out the window. It would have been an eleven-story drop and murder charges for me. I quit drinking for a couple of months.

One night in Grand Rapids, I knocked out two bikers fighting on the dance floor. Then I left the bar and my ride. Pat found me seven miles away around four in the morning, just walking down the street. I couldn't remember much at all about the last few hours or so.

Once I picked up a rock and roller by his throat with one hand and held him there until he passed out. I was drinking whiskey that night, and both he and I are lucky he's still alive. From what I understand, if all the body weight is held by the neck, it can separate the spinal cord from the brain. Only a strong neck saved that guy's life . . . and mine.

One time, on a serious binge, the three musketeers stopped at a donut shop to get some coffee. Goof said, "Looks like they're closed." Rob and I took him at his word and start relieving ourselves on the front window. When I was about done, I noticed this cop car blasting into the parking lot. The cop said that if his wife had been there, he would have cut mine off.

Luckily, Rob stayed silent while Goof started in on his "woe is me" act. "Officer, I don't know what I was thinking. I know I shouldn't be out with these two doing pranks and stuff. I tried to get in with the preppies, sir, but they threw me under the bus. We were going to a national hymn sing in Lansing a few weeks back, and we got a flat tire. Well, it was snowing something fierce and come to find out that someone stole my spare tire. Here we were in our Sunday shoes, sir. We had to walk six miles in a snowstorm before we could get help. We missed that hymn sing altogether.

"Now, Scott and Rob are crazy, sir, but they're the only friends I got. My dad's unemployed and has shingles and hemorrhoids.

My mom has a heart condition, sir, and she suffers from depression. She just sits in her chair and rocks, sir; only says about three words a day. If I go to jail again, this might make her heart stop. Sir, if you don't believe me, you go by my house. You'll see her right by the front window. Sir, I swear on the Bible that Monday morning, I'll go out first thing and buy me a new spare and find me some preppy friends. You'll never see me with these two delinquents no more." See, Goof was older and had a prior, and he put on a good performance.

I could write another hundred or more pages about my drunken mayhem, but its incredible stupidity is starting to bore me—and, I'm sure, you too. My first year in college was probably the most dangerous part of my life. By the second year, I was starting to come to my senses, having only momentary lapses into insanity, versus the last three years, which could be, more or less, described as perpetual insanity.

I ruptured two discs in my back that summer working for a landscaper near my dad's place. My left leg shriveled up, and I would frequently lose my balance and fall on campus. If I stepped just right, the nerve in my back would cut off the power to my left leg, and I would just pile up in a heap. That injury took away much of my strength and made me start thinking seriously about life. I wasn't ten foot tall and bulletproof after all. I've suffered with serious back pain ever since. Looking at my situation, it was a blessing in disguise. Maybe this was God's way of slowing me down. Kelley was at MSU with me during my second year. We were together all the time. She also had a way of slowing the crazy train down.

Chapter 8: Starting a Business and Restarting Life

A twenty-year-old guy with two ruptured discs and a landscape construction and design degree isn't getting a job with anyone. There was only one way I could stay in the profession I had come to love. There was something satisfying about building a high wall or planting a big grove of trees. If you did the job right, your name would be connected with that place as long as you breathed.

I rented an old farmhouse from my dad for $350 a month and bought a $600 pickup and some hand tools. Things were so tight that I couldn't afford insurance or license plates. We just kept dirt on the plate so you couldn't see that the stickers were old. For all the hell I'd given the police, I think they knew I was running illegally. I had to for the first two years, or I wouldn't have been able to eat. The Kentwood cops were a decent bunch. I think they knew I was struggling, and they looked the other way.

Kelley was in her final semester at MSU. One day she called me up crying, "You don't love me. You're never here. Everybody else's boyfriends are around, but I never see you."

"Baby, I'm trying to start a business. All the big companies get the good jobs. I'm just landscaping for crumbs."

"All right," she said. But she was still crying.

"I'll be right there." I had gotten a good deal on a hopped-up Kawasaki from a Vietnam vet who had been hurt in the war. I made the seventy miles in about thirty minutes.

When I walked into her dorm room, Kelley's roommate asked, "Don't you live in Grand Rapids? Didn't you just call a little while ago?"

I think the Kawasaki went over 160 mph. I don't really know.

I put a 3" x 5" card on my refrigerator that said in five years I would be worth half a million dollars. My buddies were making five to six dollars an hour, and we were eating Ramen Pride Soup. They laughed at my bold vision, but I did just that. Five years later I was worth that and more.

I worked Monday, Wednesday, and Friday for the first year because my back would lock up something fierce. On my days off, I'd put heat and ice on my back. Gradually, my strength returned. I read hundreds of books on plants and design. The economy started to go crazy when Reagan was in, and I made some decent money. The company grew fast. Kelley and I got married, but we fought a lot. I was still drinking and fighting.

I knew a local mobster who had a large bar. His uncle was part of the Saint Valentine's Day Massacre. None of his bouncers wanted to touch me. He invited me over for a few beers and showed me his mob connections. I believe he was trying to recruit me. I refused because I was already making good honest money.

My company had eight to ten guys working each summer. I was training on my heavy bag, and my strength came back to 80 percent of what it was before the disc incident in college. I was punching through cement bags and working seventy hours a week. I also built a beautiful home. My sales doubled three years in a row, and I was well on my way to making my first million.

I'd offered the crew one thousand dollars cash if they could beat me. Five different guys tried and failed. They had agreed to pay their own hospital bills in front of witnesses.

We used to have these wild parties at the old farmhouse. One day an ex-con druggie showed up and started grabbing girls' fannies. I offered the guy a beer for the road and asked him to leave. The ex-con punched me in the face. We brawled for the longest I've ever fought. Finally, I crushed in one side of his face, knocking him out. Everybody thought the guy was dead.

The punch had split my hand in half. The surgeon rebuilt it, but I had a time-sensitive wall contract to finish. I drove fifty pounds of ten-inch spikes with a sledgehammer two or three weeks after surgery. Every time I swung that hammer, I'd wince and grunt with pain. Doing this caused the pins to move inside my hand. When the surgeon removed the pins, he was horrified at how far they had shifted. When I told him about the contract, he told me to forget about the $1,400 surgery bill.

After one of these parties, Rob and I were banging around in the cornfield and woods out back with my 12 gauge loaded with birdshot. We were trying to get a pheasant or a rabbit. As we walked, Rob told me about an airplane crash movie he had just seen. A little while later, a small plane flew over.

I started into a wild-eyed routine about how I always wanted to shoot down an airplane. The plane was probably at 1,500 to 2,000 feet, but Rob was a city boy and had no idea that birdshot wouldn't get anywhere near the plane. I started banging away toward that small plane with my 12 gauge, and Rob ran away from me as fast as he could, screaming that I was a crazy man.

Kelley gave me two beautiful girls, and we only owed $40,000 on a $250,000 place. But all was not well. I started getting severe headaches, and my joints ached all the time. My big brother and I had started another landscape company in Traverse City, Michigan, and I did all the sales and design work. The company was really taking off, and we were voted Best Landscaper for their Parade of Homes that year.

That same year, we were also voted best commercial design build for the city of Holland. My brother sent me a couple of blueprints for some high-dollar homes. I couldn't focus on the paper for more than a minute before my vision blurred and my head started to ache.

Six different doctors couldn't figure out what was wrong with me. My hips and hands were starting to lock up, and my right hand started taking on a deformed appearance. The pain was unbearable. We were in a tri-level home, and just going down the short stairwell in the morning meant I had to scooch down on my butt because my hips would lock up. Later in the morning, they would loosen up and finally move, but painfully. The business went from six figures profit to four. If I was working twenty hours a week, that was good.

We had to shut down the Traverse City company and sell equipment just to live. Kelley was lucky. A job dropped in her lap, and we were able to take in a small amount of money. In eighteen months, I went from 195 pounds to 170 pounds, and maybe half the strength. In my heart, I knew that I was at death's door, but with no answers as to what, why, and where. At one time, I could carry two railroad ties 150 feet, but now I couldn't even move one.

We sold our house and built a new one in the country, paying cash for it, thirty miles north of Grand Rapids. This way, when I was dead, Kelley's life would be debt-free. I was now having ministrokes. The pain was unbearable. I'd swallow sixteen aspirins with no effect. One afternoon, just before we moved up north, I sat with a pistol to my head. Then my youngest daughter started to cry, and I went to her aid. After that, Kelley came home. The momentum had been lost; death would have to come another day.

When you know you are dying, that's when you really start thinking about eternity. I started grabbing at straws, taking home remedies, reading Jehovah's Witnesses stuff, and watching preachers on television. We had a customer with a sweet spirit, and he was one of the nicest people I had ever met. I knew he was a preacher, so I started asking him a ton of questions. His wife was sweet, too, and they helped me fill in some of the blanks I had about Christians.

I started taking heavy doses of garlic, and my condition improved. One of my wife's friends was just out of medical school. She told my wife that I had Lyme disease. I went to my doctor, and he told me there was no Lyme disease in Michigan. I told him to test for it anyway. It came back positive, but he claimed it was a bad test. If the State of Michigan said there was no Lyme disease, then, by golly, there was no Lyme disease. Yet I had been dying from it for about two years.

I called my mom. She knew a lot of people and was able to find a doctor with 120 Lyme disease patients. My second test was one of the highest he'd seen. He put me on antibiotics for two years to clean up my blood and stop the pain. Lyme disease was all over Michigan, but the State didn't want to talk about it—tourism, I suppose. Doctors believed those reports just like they believed their drug reps, and lots of people suffered because of those lies.

My old neighbor was paralyzed from the neck down from Lyme disease. In my case, it almost killed me. I hadn't left the state in ten years, so I probably got it from the swamps behind my first new home.

Lies kill and destroy, which is what the Bible says about Satan (John 10:10). I was slowly starting to believe the Bible, but I couldn't reconcile it with all the liars I'd seen in my Christian schools over the years. I had a tough time reconciling a loving God with all the pain and suffering in the world.

Then it started to make sense; just because someone says they're a Christian doesn't necessarily make it so. The mainline churches were full of people who had never really met Jesus. They never showed real faith. They were just playing the game, but Jesus said you would know them by their fruits (Matthew 7:16), that His people would do His will (Mark 3:35), and that His people are to pursue holiness (Hebrews 12:14).

I remember negotiating with God before committing my life to Christ. I asked Him if he had a campground halfway between heaven and hell with no electricity where he sent the not-totally-bad people. After all, I'd worked hard and provided well for my family. I usually told the truth. I finally concluded that the Earth had to be created by a greater power, and that if all of us lived by the principles of the Scriptures, the world would be a joyful place. The historical significance of Jesus's life and death just all added up to truth. I understood that our God is so holy that even what we consider small sins separate us from Him.

One evening, in tears, I realized that Jesus had cut through all the lies and liars. His life defined all of history. He came here to show us how to live. I was judging Jesus by people that most likely were not His. He doesn't just save people from hell; He teaches them how to live now.

I told the Lord, right then and there, that if I was going to do this Christian gig, it was going to be all out, 140 mph with no B.S. I wanted to run strong, or I wasn't even going to join the race. I gave the rest of my life to Him. It felt like when I'd thrown those two railroad ties off my shoulders back in the day. His Spirit had entered mine. He became my perfect big brother and my king that day, and He's directed my paths ever since.

I was thirty-one years old and my life of hellraising and chasing money was over.

Chapter 9: Treasure Hunting

Now, Dave was the preacher who had helped me out when I was searching. His heart was burdened for people, and he knew that most people were lost. All they have to do is ask Jesus to show them the light and He will. But people have all kinds of reasons as to why they don't call on Jesus. Mine was a load of false Christians I'd known. The bad ones discredited even the good ones in my eyes.

Dave and I pounded the streets, sometimes frantically, trying to get folks to open their eyes. This street time was the most fascinating adventure you could imagine—the incredible miracles I've seen and the things that God has taught me in the process. The first thirty-one years of my life were just like a crazy Super Bowl commercial that leads you to the main event. Satan, time and time again, had tried to destroy me, but God had answered my mom's and other relatives' prayers.

Being fearless for Satan came with its price, but it taught me to be fearless for Jesus, no matter what the cost. I'd risked my life for Satan and self, and, gradually, I learned to put both of those on the shelf. The last twenty years carry the only things of value to me now. Jesus turned a wild man into a family man, a selfish man into a giver, and a bitter man into a lover.

My hatred for lies and liars eventually led me to the truth, and the truth is that we are all like birds with broken wings. We are all damaged by selfishness and sin. When I was a young man, I didn't have all the facts and was in no position to judge anyone. Only the perfect One knows perfect truth. Remember Honeycomb—the kid I teased for his big head? He never did anything to me, but I humiliated him for a laugh. On the other hand, I hated that teacher with all my heart for roughing up another little black kid.

The truth screams out that we are all guilty before God. I can't wag my finger at anyone. Look at yourself in the mirror and be honest. Only perfect Jesus can point His finger at you and me, but what does He do? He doesn't point at us, He just holds out His hand and says come, follow me (Luke 18:22). There's a right way of living, and I'll show you the way, He says. That's what I did, and what an incredible journey I'd begun.

The Bible says that Satan loves death. Death rests in my bones, and eternal death has a hold on dozens of my old friends. But Jesus says that He gives life and life more abundantly (John 10:10). This isn't money, like some false preachers say. This is joy, peace, and love.

This life is forever, but it is also for today. One of the first times we did street ministry, Dave took me into the hood. He drove a blue Chevy sedan, and we were both clean-cut. We had no way of knowing that the house we stopped at was a drug house, and they thought we were cops. People started jumping out the back windows. Two young Latinos, the drug dealer's son and his girlfriend, came out and sat on the neighbor's porch.

Three young blacks came up to us on the sidewalk. They were wearing long black coats. I figured they were packing. I think the drug dealer sent them out to slow us down while they hid the drugs. Dave started right in, telling them about Jesus, asking them if they had ever sinned.

The one fellow said, "Oh, no," while the other two chuckled.

Dave remained persistent. "You mean you've never lied?"

"Oh, no."

"You mean you've never stolen?"

"Oh, no."

"You mean you never disobeyed your parents?"

"Oh, no."

"You mean you never lusted after a woman?"

"Oh, no."

At that I interjected, "Oh, he's one of those queers."

His buddies started laughing. This banger started getting in my face, and I told him, "You don't know who you're dealing with, man. You better just settle down." Dave began turning red, and they all started cussing at us while they headed down the sidewalk.

Then the two teenagers came from the neighbor's porch and asked, "Hey, what were you talking about?" Dave led those two to Christ that week. It was incredible, this whole circus we had to wade through to get to those kids, but God knew those two were curious about His Son. God had directed our steps that day (Proverbs 3:6). I would see this over and over. One time, Dave and I brought flowers to a prostitute after her john sliced opened her guts. We pleaded for her to get off the crazy train before it was too late.

Dave could probably write a book of his own with thousands of stories like this. God has used this man all over the country and all over the world to lead people to a personal relationship with Jesus. Dave just wants heaven to be full. He's not leading people to a collection plate. He asks the brick-and-mortar church people, and flashy, puffed-up preachers the same questions he asks the drug dealers on the street. Your traditions, your education, and all the letters behind your name mean nothing. Only when Jesus sits on the throne of your heart are you free from sin and death.

However, there was trouble in paradise. Dave was a preacher at a small church, but on numerous occasions he mentioned that the Lord had called him to be an evangelist. Time and again, Dave would be out doing street ministry, and we would be in long conversations with someone who was searching for the truth. Then, we'd get in the car, and he'd say, "Well, I was supposed to meet someone from church for lunch and look, now it's 4:00."

There were people in the church for whom he was supposed to be a pastor, and he was neglecting them. It was plain to me that the Lord had called Dave to be an evangelist, but his wife had called him to be a preacher. I told him so. As much as I loved Dave, I felt like I was enabling him, and it was time to find another church where the preacher was called by God to preach. God gives us specific gifts, some as preachers and some as evangelists (Ephesians 4:11).

This was the beginning of a long journey that, to some extent, I'm still on twenty years later. I'm not sure that I'll ever find a man who has been called to preach with the same pureness and zeal as Dave. Six months after I told Dave we were looking for another church, Dave did step down as the preacher. He has been an evangelist ever since. I am so blessed to be able to call Dave my friend. We thank the Lord for both Dave and his wife, especially the time they spent with me, answering all my questions before I jumped with all my heart into God's Kingdom.

One of Dave's good friends was a fiery preacher in the South. I went down there to help them build an orphanage. We fell in love with their family, and together we did some pro-life street ministry. This group would cover a bus with Scriptures and stand with pictures of aborted babies in front of abortion clinics.

I had a man in an old pickup slam his driver's door into me at about 25 mph while I was holding up a pro-life sign. We've had skinheads threaten us and county workers throw coke bottles at us, while the cops did nothing.

The Billings, Montana police arrested a friend of mine just for handing out pro-life literature in front of an abortion clinic on a kill day. The folks who stand up for these innocent little babies take an incredible amount of abuse from Satan and his people.

If you rescue a woman from being raped and kill the man in the process, you'll be a front-page hero. Try to save an innocent child from a brutal murder, and you're a politically incorrect zero. American minds have become terribly twisted.

One time, a group from this Southern church got jumped by several deathscorts—people who commit violence on behalf of their cause. Some of the boys got beaten up. There was a sweet group of elderly Catholic ladies who used to pray in front of the clinic. One of the deathscorts shoved one of the elderly ladies into the street. The cops watched and did nothing to protect them. That's what started the brawl, and my friends came to her aid.

One of the pro-life protestors was dragged by his beard down the pavement by a deathscort. The pro-life group felt that they needed some of my punching skills to protect them, so the preacher asked me to come down and show those country boys how to break things with their fists. A few months later one of the boys used my defensive punching techniques to knock out a gang leader about a hundred pounds heavier than him who had assaulted their group. He did this with one punch.

Later, they took me to the scene of the crime, and my justice meter went off. I started yelling at the cops. I figured a few of them were probably some of the same cops who just stood by and watched while this church group got pummeled. I took a 3' x 3' picture of an aborted baby in front of those cruisers and hollered, "Serve and protect, serve and protect!" over and over again at the top of my lungs. I watched their faces, and some of the cops were ashamed. But some of their faces were full of hate. They didn't get out of their cruisers. Maybe they thought I had the jawbone of an ass in my pocket (see Samson in Judges 15:16). The cops sent for two women officers, who tailed me the entire day.

One of the boys pointed out the leader of the deathscorts who started the riots. He was probably six foot six and had a red bandana on his head. I stood in his way on the sidewalk. I think he knew that I would destroy him if he touched me, so he walked around me. The deathscorts were peaceful that day, walking down the sidewalk, escorting those girls to kill their babies. *The blind leading the blind*, I thought.

Those poor people are just believing the lie that abortion isn't murder, just like I did for thirty-one years. Poor babies. Nobody knows for sure whether they'll go to heaven or hell. I sure paid for my father's sins, but I really hope that those babies don't. They never even had a chance to sin. May God have mercy on those babies first, their mothers and their fathers and their deathscorts next.

There is great power in the name of Jesus, as I was soon to find out. Dave was preaching down south at Brother John's church, and I went along. They had an outdoor preaching area that they used in the summer.

Their church had thirty-three bullet holes in it, and the visiting missionary with four or five kids had three or four bullet holes in his trailer too. The local police did little to protect them.

The church was infuriated over all the gunfire that had been directed at the building. An aggressively pro-life church under attack doesn't get much press. You would think it would, but, no, these were white, rural, aggressively pro-life Baptists. They could hardly get a police report. Does anyone else have their justice meter going off?

While Dave was preaching at night, just after dark, a dark blue mud truck dropped off four or five men at the top of the hill, perhaps 150 yards away. Then, this truck shut off its lights and took off. Four or five men from the church ran across the field, and another small group ran up the hill by way of the dirt road.

Before you could say yee-haw twice, there must have been ten guns out, from a congregation of fifty people.

Now, I had never missed a good fight in my life. Even though I didn't have a gun, I always carried a knife. That blade had saved my neck twice already, and three times is a charm, don't they say?

As I ran on the open road, I thought, *those are probably a bunch of drunk hillbillies and they're going to open fire*, so I jumped into the woods. The grade of the woods was much higher than the road, which gave me a view of most of the men. I realized that if the men on the road started shooting toward the hill, the other church members would be caught in the crossfire.

I jumped down the road ahead of the guys and charged up the hill while I yelled, "I rebuke you scumbags in the name of Jesus Christ!" When I made it to the top, I only found two young men, and they were walking around in a daze, almost like a pair of dumb calves.

I'd known a preacher who, in the name of Jesus, had rebuked a man who was swinging a baseball bat at him, and the man just collapsed in a daze, similar to these two. Now, I have no way of knowing for sure, but I believe those two were possessed by demons. I believe they dropped their guns in the woods and wandered to the road. The others, who weren't possessed, escaped through the woods when they saw our small army coming.

Brother John got a big kick out of me coming to a gun fight with a knife and catching those two guys. I don't care what you carry, if you can't call on Jesus, you haven't got anything. Jesus's name chases the demons out of men. Jesus stormed the gates of hell, and he kicked in Satan's door. Jesus rules heaven and hell, and now Satan is just playing out the last few cards he's been given.

Jesus won't force anyone to come to Him. He's not a brutal dictator like Satan. Jesus just lovingly holds out His hands and says, "Hey, come my way. Are you ready to leave the insanity? Come with me. Help me build something that will last forever. How long are you going to spend building sandcastles with Satan? Why don't you help me fill my real castle that my Father built for me in heaven?

"Some of these people you tell about me are going to be your best buddies forever in a perfect place and in a perfect world. No more lies or liars, and no more pain. Please, just kick over that sandcastle—or whatever it is that takes way too much of your time and energy—and follow me. Do my will. I love you.

I died for you. My plan for your life is perfect, now get the sand out of your shoes and your shorts.

"Just brush all that worldly sand off, follow me to peace, true love, and paradise. Here's a fast white horse (Holy Spirit power) for you, cowboy. Hang on, and don't look back. The road is narrow. Stay on it, and it will take you home."

Those people down South are the sweetest people you'll meet in your whole life. The power of God just hums in their little congregation.

Who knows how many young ladies decided to keep their babies when they heard the truth from this church group? Whereas that lying abortion nurse just counsels that it is a blob of tissue. Well, it sure looks like a baby to me.

In the few short years my wife and I have done this, I'd say there are at least nine people walking this earth who wouldn't be here if we hadn't helped their parents change their minds and keep their babies.

Think about it. For thirty-one years, people I knew and influenced were dying all around me, and Satan was using my friends to fill his burning hell hole. Now, Jesus saves my soul, and I'm out there on the streets, planting seeds that will save lives here and for heaven. God's ways are incredible. What a great and glorious God I serve.

Chapter 10: The Fellowship Days

We started going to a Brethren Fellowship. This congregation didn't believe in paid preachers, based on the writings of Paul who said he worked with his own hands so as not to damage the cause of Christ (Acts 20:33–35 and 1 Corinthians 9:15–19). Paul wrote fourteen books of the Bible and started many churches, but he provided for himself and those with him by making tents.

I see this model as purer and more advantageous to believers. I've lost count of the people I've spoken to who will have nothing to do with God because the "church is all about money."

At the Brethren Fellowship, we had a group of elders who ran the service, and the church members looked out for each other. One of the men, who struggled with heavy drinking, damaged a bridge with his truck, and seemed to have trouble managing his affairs. A few times, this spilled over into the group, causing discord.

The Brethren Fellowship services were neat. The elders would just share what God had done or had laid on their hearts for that week. One of the older elders thought that every one of the men should wear suits and ties, which didn't go over well, and he graciously backed down. There were disputes about head coverings and other things related to church order.

But after a while, I felt it was becoming too much of a holy huddle. Bernie was the eldest, and he agreed with me. We tried to witness to his neighbors but with little success. I suppose the neighbors believed the fellowship was weird.

We've been spoon-fed the mainline brick-and-mortar, professional Christian modality for so long that anything else looks, to them, like a cult. Not so in China, where there is no long history of professional Christianity. They base their organization only on the Bible, which speaks many times about meeting in homes. I have heard that China has some eighty million people attending home churches, likely to avoid persecution. I believe it would be good for America, but we'll probably never see it.

Most Americans who claim to be Christians are steeped in traditions but only have a shallow understanding of God's Word. These traditions keep them hitched to controlling preachers or priests. They often follow them instead of just following Jesus, who said for us to pick up our cross and follow Him (Matthew 16:24 and Luke 14:27).

Bernie used to call me the zealot. He was so cool and shrewd that I never knew if he meant it as a compliment or a kick in the pants. He was a knowledgeable gentleman. The way he loved his wife and took care of her when she suffered through Alzheimer's was a blessing to see. They are both with Jesus now. I really loved Bernie and the others, but the church overflowed with discord, and some of the women were being rather catty, as well.

Despite that, it was one of my best times as a Christian—other than when I didn't attend church at all for over two years after our next few church stops.

———

When I was at the Fellowship, I bought an ambulance and put Scripture verses, pro-life signs, and pro-second amendment stuff on the outside. Inside, we stuffed all the racks where the medical supplies were stored with Christian tracts and literature to hand out to people. We had great fun with that ambulance. We took it to special events. I remember the first time I drove it with all the Scriptures on it. The thought of being seen in it made me feel nervous, like, "Everyone's looking at me," "I better not speed," and "Be holy."

I'm reminded of those stuck-up people at church that helped put me on a roller coaster that almost took me to hell. Guess what, fellow Christians, everyone is looking, and not many are impressed with what they see. How many people will be in hell because you're the only Christian they knew, and they didn't want to be like you?

This thought scares me because God delivered me from the drinking right away, but it took Him twenty years to kill my temper. The temper had helped me survive in the hood, and I considered it a strength. I fell for another lie from Satan, and you know the Bible says that Satan loves death (John 10:10).

Well, that temper killed relationships, and it almost killed me and a sorry liar who stole a lot of my money (a story I cover in a few chapters). It took a great deal of suffering for me to finally realize that my temper was my biggest weakness.

We had the ambulance detailed with Scriptures like Psalm 139 and a large picture of my then-youngest daughter sleeping in a cloth diaper, to promote pro-life ethics. We used the loudspeaker at times to preach at different venues.

Al Gore came to Grand Rapids when he was running for president. The public schools, of course, brought bus load after bus load of young children to this political event. The media reported that the crowd was around 5,000. I parked the ambulance at the entrance so all the Al Gore fans would have to view the pro-life message.

A friend promised to help me. He spent about five minutes there, got scared, and took off. I spent the whole morning talking to various people by myself, explaining why it was immoral to advocate the murder of innocent children in the womb. Mr. Gore himself claimed to be pro-life until he stepped on the national scene. I am sure that at some point he realized that being pro-life would limit his political options.

Walking the streets with a sandwich sign, I was verbally accosted by a pro-choice lady who was sporting a marine butch cut. She kept harassing me and arguing with me about the various points of legal abortion and how a woman has the right to murder her child as long as it is inside her body. She had half a dozen feminists who followed her around hooting at me.

These women simply refused to see that the child at twenty weeks was almost fully formed and certainly fully human. Then

I remembered that a friend of mine had given me a picture of an aborted baby at twenty-four weeks. I found this picture on my clipboard, and I showed it to these brainwashed girls. Everyone except the leader gasped, horrified at the picture of a real-life abortion. I explained this was what they were promoting here, and it was plain to see that it was murder. All the girls took off without a word, except their leader. She glared at me and stated, "Can we just agree to disagree?"

I said, "No, ma'am, you advocate the murder of innocents. That's a crime, and you and your friends all know it."

By now, Al Gore was getting ready to speak, and I wanted to heckle him. The UAW boys, standing on the marble steps of some government building, commanded the best view of the podium. That left me about a ten-foot opening at the top of the steps to heckle from. As I climbed the steps, a big, long-haired UAW boy pushed me backward. As he shoved me, I grabbed his collar and planted my left foot under the lip of the top step. This two-hundred-and-fifty-pound dude flew over my head, face first to the cement below. It was a perfectly executed judo move that left me unharmed, but with two state boys taking me to their cruiser.

As they were about to arrest me, one of Al Gore's Secret Service men said, "Hey fellas, the long-haired guy tried to shove him down the stairs. He was just defending himself." The cops let me go but did nothing to long hair. The Secret Service guy said to me, "Thanks, you're doing the right thing. And by the way, somebody stuck an Al Gore sign to the back of your sign." I thanked him, ripped it up, and approached the ten-foot opening again. The crowd was growing silent so Al could speak. I yelled at the top of my lungs, for all to hear, "Al Gore is a baby murdering scumbag," and I left.

We eventually gave the ambulance to another pro-life friend. He took it all over the country, even to the Olympics in Utah. It was becoming clear to me that the public schools were Satan's throne in America. The schools have had a consistent record of undermining freedom and morality for some time. My street ministry would focus more on the schools, while the Lord told Kelley to drop the pro-life ministry.

My dad was incredibly wealthy, but he was headed for hell. He was an incredible control freak. He wanted me to run his company, but I wasn't interested. To get back at me, when Kelley and I were starting out, he told all his rich friends that my business was too busy. The reality was that we were starving. I almost beat him in a bar soon after finding this out. But we patched our relationship up after I became a Christian.

I called him one day and said, "Dad, you're going to hell. You need Jesus. It's not just head knowledge. Satan believes in Jesus. You need a personal relationship with Him. You have too much money and think you don't need God. So, I'm praying that you will go bankrupt."

Two years later his company was gone, and he had given his life to Jesus after two near-death experiences. He called Kelley, in tears, and said how he now knew what Scott meant about Jesus.

Just before I left the Fellowship, I started going to college campuses, trying to reach out to the students. That's been one of the biggest blessings of my life. I love talking to these kids who are struggling in an America that is clearly in a state of moral and financial decline. Most of them know they'll never have the opportunity that their parents had, but they are trying to make the most of it. It's refreshing to see these kids with their eyes wide open, trying to make the best of life.

Most of them are willing to talk if they have the time. They're not so set in their ways that they can't change the course of their lives in a better direction, with God's guidance, of course, and a bit of encouragement from me. I'm currently helping a young man start his first business, and I'm blessed to do so. I met him at one of my favorite colleges.

Before I get too far off track, I have to take you on my journey to find the perfect church for my family.

Chapter 11: The Country Church and the Little Chapel

I started going to a small country church. It had this little jumpy preacher. He was an excellent administrator, and he had a wonderful kid's ministry. But I was starting to think, *here we go again*. God's given him gifts, but they weren't leadership and preaching. He's just another guy who the Lord led to ministry, and his wife led to preaching.

We volunteered at the youth home, which is a jail for minors. One day, I gave my testimony to the kids, and four of them wanted to accept Jesus as their Savior. This preacher came up to the kids and frantically started telling them that they could only get saved once. But the power of God had convicted them of their sins, and two of the kids were even crying. This pastor had been working there a while and had seen next to nothing happen. Now, this guy breezes in, and four kids just jump into Jesus's arms.

Deep down inside, he was horrified, and I could see it. Here's a guy who's enamored with his title and wants to control everything. He should be jumping for joy that Jesus used this new guy to pull four kids out of hell. Praise God! He could think to himself, "Wow, God really has His hands on this guy. Thank you, God, for placing him here. We're going to reach hundreds of hurting kids."

After we left the building, I sat in my car, crying about what a wonderful thing I'd just witnessed. But I couldn't help thinking that the pastor was jealous of me because of the gift God had given me. My spiritual leader was just another clean-cut climber. I knew right then we were heading down the wrong road.

Soon after that, we started attending another small country church, the little chapel. The pastor had a good attitude, and he wasn't so controlling. We plugged in one hundred percent, and I became their volunteer youth director. The church had structural problems because the elders were two women and one man; their kids didn't follow God closely. According to Scripture, these three didn't qualify as elders (1 Timothy 3:1–13).

I knew this but didn't think it would matter. This elder structure, however, ended up causing a huge crisis in the church that divided and hurt many members. The Lord showed me that whenever a church or a member diverges from the instruction manual Jesus gave us—the New Testament—troubles eventually follow.

The crisis that precipitated my leaving the brick-and-mortar church started with two troubled teens we had worked with. They were two adopted girls that came from different families. Both girls had come from troubled homes and had been removed from their birth families.

One of the girls was adopted into a wealthier, solid Christian family that ran the children's Sunday school program. The other child was adopted into a more worldly home. The adopted girl from the wealthier home made some accusations against the other family which, I counseled the pastor, were probably false. A month or so later, the pastor verbally abused the accused family and kicked them out of the church.

The young girl showed up at my youth group on Wednesday and sat bawling in the kitchen. The horror of this situation was that this girl had just given her life to Jesus. Satan had used the weak elder structure and the weak pastor to destroy this girl's faith. I understand she is currently practicing witchcraft.

While we were there, the Holy Spirit began to speak to me on a regular basis. One day, I was about to go deer hunting, and the Lord said, "You've hunted enough, spend more time with the kids." I did, for about a week. Then we had a beautiful day and a fresh snow.

I had a huge pine tree that overlooked forty acres. The tree stand was thirty-two feet up that pine. The sun was out, and there was no wind. I grabbed my gun and gear and climbed the pine. The branches were icy. I had been up there for an hour or so when huge gusts of wind started shaking the tree something fierce. I decided to climb down, but my hand slipped, and I fell thirty-two feet, knocking myself out while taking out two branches.

I don't know how long I lay on the ground, nor how I walked to the car and loaded myself and my bent gun into the car. I don't even remember driving to a friend's house less than a mile away. I do remember I broke a few ribs and had a concussion.

The Bible says that the Lord chastises the ones He loves (Revelation 3:19). Deer hunting was an idol to me, and God had told me to stop hunting. One year, I hunted thirty-five days and let twenty bucks go because they weren't big enough. Trophy bucks had become an obsession.

Jesus didn't mind my hunting. He was just teaching me balanced living. The funny thing was that my back pain had healed up for some time after the fall. I viewed it as a miracle, but the pain eventually came back. Fortunately, the obsession with horns never did. I still love the woods and hunting, but I think we hunted six full days last year. I shot a doe for meat. But I read the whole New Testament during deer season, and it blessed me more than any set of horns could. It was time spent with Jesus, studying His ways. I was also able to help a couple of my neighbors.

Around this time, my father died under horrid circumstances. I was in a rage about it for years. I'd cry in my bedroom to the Lord to help me, but I heard nothing from him for two years. I finally came to the end of my rage, and I read in God's Word warning us to not withhold forgiving (Matthew 6:15). I forgave everyone involved, and the Lord started directing my paths again.

Well, we left the little chapel and its troubles behind, and I didn't attend church for about two years. It was the most incredible part of my Christian life. God used all these bumps in the church road to force me to search myself and the Scriptures and to become obedient to Him. He spoke to me almost daily. He would direct my paths . . . literally, left, now right, okay, right again.

Kelley and I sent letters to fifty-eight churches—every church within thirty miles of our home. I explained how we went door to door with gospel booklets, telling everyone about Jesus. I offered to meet with the elders of their churches so that we could devise a plan to canvass their neighborhoods with God's Word. I could supply the literature and use my gas; it would cost them nothing. For months, we heard nothing. I bought around 10,000 booklets and just started out on my own. I was going to hit every home in the county, which I believe was 55,000, with gospel booklets.

I remember telling this woman at a laundromat how Jesus had changed my life. She looked like she was going to accept Jesus as her Savior, but I had to admit to her that I couldn't think of one church around there to send her to. I told her the decision would ultimately have to be between her and Jesus.

A pastor of a church about a half an hour away with about twenty Christians called me. He had received the letter and said that the Lord had told him to call. We had canvassed his neighborhood and visited his church many times, but I had never felt we should be there permanently.

However, we enjoyed a wonderful relationship in the Lord. My children liked taking classes from him in Shinsei Kenpo (a self-defense martial art), and he officiated at one of my daughter's wedding. It has been a blessing to know someone else who listens to the Holy Spirit. He is now a missionary in Brazil.

This booklet ministry began in late 2006. By 2009 we had hit just about every house in the areas we were targeting. For two of those years, I wasn't going to church at all, and we handed out at least 70,000 "Help from Above" booklets.

Because of their lack of interest, I've concluded that most big churches aren't really looking to bring the lost to Jesus. They spend most of their efforts trying to steal members from other congregations. They spend their budgets on fancier buildings and more entertainment. They consistently become more of an unholy huddle as they focus more on the numbers than on living God's truth. It's what I call the "business model church." In fact, most of them don't have elders like in Acts. No, they're so slick that they have a board of directors, just like Wall Street and the banks.

Chapter 12: Direct Your Paths

While driving one day, the Lord said, "You've been chasing landscape work two days a week. Will you do *my* work two days a week?" I said yes, so I would get up and drive to wherever the Lord led me. One day I was close to Kalamazoo, and the Lord instructed me to go down a drive and talk to a woman I would find there. I went down a long drive and found a woman who had just been fired.

She was an alcoholic and had lost her nursing job. I explained the gospel to her. She took one of my booklets and hugged me real tight, in tears. We talked for an hour. God knew her need, and He used me to warm her heart while she was in despair.

She had no car but claimed she had a daughter who lived close by, though the daughter wasn't much help. I told her I would try to find her a car. A few weeks later, her daughter got her a car. I've always thought that my generous offer shamed her daughter into helping her mother.

Who better to do this kind of work than a former drunk like me? The number of alcoholics I've talked to is way out of proportion to any other sin problem that I've encountered on the street. I don't think that's weird, considering the Bible says that God will direct our paths (Proverbs 3:5–6).

Every day was something different. One day, He'd send me to a small town and garage sales. The next day, He'd send me somewhere different. Once, He had me go to a nail salon. Boy, I felt out of place, but I obeyed Him.

My kids would use a yellow marker to highlight the streets where we had already left tracts. One day, the Lord said, "Go to Franklin Street." I said that we'd already done that, and I kept going to the next house, praying for the families in it. The Lord said, "No, I won't answer your prayers. I told you to go to Franklin Street."

I started running back to Franklin Street. My daughter Amanda ran with me. Right at the corner sat a bunch of teenagers. They all received the gospel. I'm thinking, "Look how much God loves these people. He has me running four blocks to make sure they have the roadmap to find Him. There He is again, holding out His nail-pierced hand and asking, 'Come to Paradise, my friend.'" It was incredible to see those young people right at the beginning of Franklin Street.

We finished the rest of the county and started on another county, sometimes with Dave's help. As you may recall, Dave is the man who led me to Christ and who had left preaching to become a full-time evangelist.

By this time, the economy had collapsed, and I was running out of money, so I was careful about my driving. My wife was telling me to slow down, but I felt that I couldn't let God down.

One morning, the Lord told me to go see Mrs. Roe. I searched for and found a Mrs. Roe in the Grand Rapids phone book.

So I could save on gas, I told the Lord I would witness to her on another day when I was already going to Grand Rapids. A couple weeks later, I planned to head to Mrs. Roe's. The problem was that my wife had purged the old phone books, throwing away the one that had her address in it, and she was not in the new book. I was getting frantic and started feeling guilty, but then I found another Mrs. Roe in Richland.

I got in my truck and went immediately to that address. I arrived at her door to find her not home, but, to my amazement, her house was in front of the only trailer park we had missed in Allegan County. The Lord was smiling on me that day as He did this little miracle to make sure we had done a thorough job. He was holding out His hand to everybody, and He was clearly showing me His deep love for everyone.

We are all free to choose heaven or hell. He's not putting anyone in a headlock, but He wants everyone who is truly searching for the truth to find it. I know that I'll be hanging out with someone from that trailer park in heaven someday.

We were at Pizza Hut with family. I watched a disheveled, impoverished-looking older woman ask the young lady at the counter how much it would cost for a cup of water. The cashier answered rudely that it would be twenty-five cents. The older woman responded with a look of sadness that pricked my heart. She dug in her purse for quite some time, which made me feel all the worse for her. She got her water and quickly left. Following her out the door, I grabbed a simple gospel booklet from my car, and slipped a fifty-dollar bill in the middle of it.

I was trying to show her that Jesus earnestly loved her and that I cared for her. I wanted her to see that the entire world wasn't coarse and mean. She thanked me and started looking inside the booklet. While I was returning to the restaurant she shouted out, "Sir, this is yours. You left some money in here." I told her that it was for her, and that Jesus loved her. What a pure, poor, honest person. How many people would have tried to return my money? In a nation full of climbers, she blessed me more than I blessed her. God had truly changed me.

My daughter Katie and I were canvassing Grand Rapids. We got into a system where we could feel the Lord leading us. We were driving down a street in a rough neighborhood, asking God to direct our paths. Grand Rapids has almost a million people, and we couldn't hit every home there. But God knew who was really looking for truth. As we drove, I told Katie that Coleman must be the street. As we drove down Coleman, Katie said, "Look at all those apartments."

There was a man walking across the lot who looked really scary—tattoos everywhere. I said something like, "Here we go, kid, thrown into the fire." I approached the man. "Good morning, sir. Got something for you, and Jesus is the real deal, sir."

He started in at once. "What's all this about Jesus, man? Look, you need to meet my wife. You see, I haven't worked in over two years. Now, my wife's sister is a Christian. A while ago, she started praying that I get a job. I was just headed to my first day of my new job, and then you show up, man. I'll certainly read this, but I gotta run. I don't wanna be late for my first day. Thanks."

Katie and I talked to his wife for a little while after he left. God was clearly calling this man home, like He did me. This guy knew it wasn't an accident. God had gotten him a new job. I just gave him the scriptural tools to find that relationship with his big heavenly brother, Jesus.

Chapter 13: More Ministry Opportunities

For about twelve years, we volunteered at the Grand Rapids Home for Veterans. Some of these men were the greatest guys I've ever met, and some were the most selfish and deranged. We adopted an old Catholic gentleman, nicknamed Joe. We loved him, and he genuinely loved our kids. He had a special place in His heart for my most rebellious child.

Joe had deep scars from WWII, especially the Battle of the Bulge in France. Two of his friends were next to him when a German shell hit the barn where they were sleeping. Both of his friends died and were buried near a small church in France. Later he requested to be buried next to his friends when he died, but the French wouldn't have it. I don't think he ever reconciled his hatred for the church and the death of two good men. I think, in a way, he blamed God for both.

Joe was so scarred from the war that he never married. I hope to see him in heaven, but he was so stoic. "If you confess with your mouth the Lord Jesus and believe in your heart that God has raised Him from the dead, you will be saved" (Romans 10:9). I'm not sure if he ever really gave his life to the Lord, and I don't believe I ever heard him say Jesus's name.

I'd tell him that amid all the wickedness of the world, God had given him a family that loved him, and none of this would have happened if I hadn't met Christ. God's goodness shines through all the mess if you are willing to look for it.

After serving at the veterans home for eleven years, I was asked to preach at the chapel on Sunday evenings, but I never felt like I was any good at it. Being asked by a man and being called by the Holy Spirit are two different things altogether, yet I did agree to their request.

One gentleman named Alan gave his life to the Lord one night while I was preaching. What a blessing to have known him. He was a great storyteller and had a sweet loving spirit.

The devil would show his face occasionally while we ministered. There was a guy there who threatened to do things to my teenage girls. He would hide in the halls and shut off the lights as my kids walked through. Then he would stand there and just leer at them. One evening, I had had enough. I told him that if he ever touched one of my kids, I would gut him like a pig. He never bothered us again.

There was another man there by the name of Lamar. One evening, he came to the service and wept almost the entire time. I spoke with him afterward. He was in three major battles, one of which had been made into a movie. He just kept crying and crying, saying, "None of my friends made it off that hill." What do you say to this poor guy? He was thrown into the fire; the smell of blood and smoke never left him. He didn't sneak out of the Vietnam War like so many others did.

These guys were incredibly needy, and sometimes I wouldn't get home until one o'clock in the morning. I felt like I couldn't do street ministry, run my business, raise my kids, and continue to preach. Furthermore, I had never been in a war. Somebody that had seen it firsthand would have to be called to their aid. This was not my gift or calling. I stepped down after about a year of preaching.

Another thing that has really stuck with me is a man they called Max. He walked with a cane. I believe he was hit by a phosphorus bomb in Vietnam. Most of his face was blown off, and he was blind, but he used to come to the chapel once in a while and sing praises to God with an incredible voice. Even after all his suffering, he sang praises for our God. That's what man was made for.

I continued putting in my two days, as the Lord had requested in the spring of the year. Katie and I were on the streets, and the Lord told me to go to Holland. It was Tulip Time, and I knew the place would be crawling with stuck-up yuppies. I argued with God out loud as we approached Holland. "Lord, do I really have to do this? Please Lord, I don't want to witness to all these snobs." As we approached Holland, the Holy Spirit told me to go right, then right again, and finally right again.

We were now heading north, away from the festival, to one of the largest trailer parks I've ever seen. Most of the parks have "No Soliciting" signs on them. We just prayed that God would blind anyone that would oppose us and lead us to those who were really searching for the truth. We dropped close to five hundred booklets that day.

As we approached the last five or six trailers, we noticed a man leaning against his rust bucket truck, parked in front of one of the worst-looking trailers in the park. His name was Chris. He had just recently lost his job, along with about a million other Michigan families. He was an ex-military guy who had been stabbed in the neck while working at a party store in Flint. He found himself laid low and had given his life to Jesus, much the same way I had. And guess what? He used to have a terrible drinking problem like mine.

We talked like old friends for the next half hour. Just as I was getting ready to leave, he said, "Hey Scott, would you please pray for me? I'm trying to stop smoking, and my adopted son just beat up some kid real bad. They had to pin his hips together. You see, my adopted son's been trying to have contact with his birth father, but his birth father won't give him the time of day. The kid is just full of anger. I don't know what to do with him."

The Lord told me to open my wallet. I had three twenties and a fifty. I was thinking about giving him a twenty, but the Lord thought otherwise. I gave Chris the fifty with one more gospel booklet. The Holy Spirit then gave me great words of wisdom for Chris. I told him to tell his boy that he chose him as his son and he loved him, and his Heavenly Father loved him more than he could. Take the boy out somewhere special, buy him the best steak in town, and tell him how Jesus has changed you from your old drunken ways.

Chris said, "No, you can't give me this money. You're going to make me cry, brother."

To which I responded, "No I'm not, bro. I'm out of here."

Katie finished dropping booklets for the remainder of the trailers. As we got to the truck, she said, "Dad, he's lying on the hood of his truck, crying."

"Don't stare. Let's go. We're going to see Chris and his son someday in heaven. Some days street ministry sure is intense."

I was so flustered I didn't even realize I was driving down the street the wrong way. Katie started laughing at me. "Yeah, Dad. Your driving sure is intense."

We handed out booklets at almost five hundred trailers, but we only had one meaningful conversation, and Chris was it. It wasn't a coincidence, my friends. God had directed me to Chris's door at the exact time that Chris stepped outside for a cigarette. God knew that Chris's boy needed to be pulled out of that pit of bitterness, and God knew that witnessing His power and timing would encourage both Katie and me.

Chapter 14: Gangbangers

I owned an incredible motorcycle—a Suzuki TL1000R with a chameleon paint job. Depending on the light and the angle that you looked at the bike, the paint would appear to change colors. It had a top speed of about 170 mph. I got up there a few times. God had cured me of drinking, but not yet the speed thing. I was talking with the Lord one day and told Him, "Maybe I should sell that bike and get something more appropriate for ministry."

The Lord said, "You're more effective with that bike."

A month or so later, I was at a construction site, handing out dozens of booklets to the workers. One guy said, "I don't need one. My name is Jehovah."

The way he mocked God took my breath away. As I got on the bike, I prayed, "Lord, rebuke that man in front of all those men for mocking you." The Lord told me he would, with such force that it felt like I had been punched in the chest. I felt like the Lord was going to kill him. I was compelled to pray, "Please, don't kill him."

A little while after that, the Lord sent me to my old neighborhood. I hadn't been there in probably twenty-five years. I stopped and talked to a young black man. He was totally in love with my bike. Now I understood what God was trying to tell me about my motorcycle. He wasn't sending me to yuppies. I'd run with a rough crowd, and that was where he was sending me. I told the young man how Jesus had changed my heart.

As he was leaving, I said, "Make sure you read that thing today. You don't know what a day might bring around here. You're liable to be shot by some crackhead on your way home."

He assured me he would. "You're right about the crackheads," he said.

I drove to the worst part of town, just waiting for the Holy Spirit to lead me to my next stop. There were about half a dozen black men who looked like older gang leaders. These guys were drinking beer on the front porch at about ten o'clock in the morning, and God told me to talk to them. I told the group, "The Lord told me to talk to you."

One guy said, "Did you say the Lord?"

"Yes, I did."

He then started a long story about some preacher who picked him up in a rainstorm, paid his cell phone bill, and bought him dinner. This preacher said that the Lord told him to do it.

By then, the gang leader had had enough with this guy's story. He said, "Shut the f*** up," and sent this guy down the road, just by pointing his finger. Now I knew who was in charge. I started telling this leader how Jesus had changed me.

Another guy says, "Hey, you got any work?"

I said, "No, my business has been real slow since the crash. I don't know anybody who's hiring." He shoved the tract I had given him into the pocket of my shirt, almost ripping my pocket off in the process. Then he took off down the road.

The leader's name was Johan. He started taking off his shirt, saying, "I don't show this to just anyone." A huge angel tattoo covered his whole back. The angel was carrying a pistol, bent over, execution style. Just his way of telling me he's a shooter, I guess. Then he said, "Let me tell you about my god, Muhammad."

The Lord told me that it was time to go. I said, "Johan, I've got business to take care of on the north side of town. If the Lord tells me to come back, I will, and we'll talk about it then."

He got all riled up and started cursing. I walked to my bike, and, as I started it up, I saw the whole gang coming down the street, walking like a dozen Nazis, two abreast. The weird thing was that these men all looked like they were the same size. The man that was leading them was the fellow that almost ripped my shirt. My bike was running.

I rode about a block and a half, and there was the young man that the preacher picked up, waving the booklet and smiling at me. He believed in the Lord now, I was sure. God's been using His obedient people to hunt him down. "But, beloved, do not forget this one thing, that with the Lord one day is as a thousand years, and a thousand years as one day. The Lord is not slack concerning His promise, as some count slackness, but is longsuffering toward us, not willing that any should perish but that all should come to repentance" (2 Peter 3:8–9).

I spoke to the Lord, saying, "Johan got in my face. I don't want him thinking I'm afraid of him. I'll go back right now. I've never taken a beating for you yet."

The Holy Spirit answered, "No, Johan wants to kill you."

Two weeks later I returned with a gift card to a good steak house, and Johan was shocked. The conversation went something like this:

"Johan, the Lord told me to come back and give you one of these. I wish I could go have a steak with you, but I can't stay long. Hey, who's your friend? Hello, Mike. My name is Scott, got a gospel booklet for you."

Mike responded, "Thanks, I got a ministry too, but I gotta go," as he darted in the house.

Johan started to get in my face again. He said, "My dad don't like white people. He's like seventy years old and got nothing to lose. If he sees you on the front porch, he might shoot you."

"All right then." I moved down the road, calling back, "See you later, Lord willing." And that was the last time I saw him. As I left Johan's, I said under my breath, "Lord, have Mike leave that booklet where the old man can find it. Let Jesus change his bitter heart like He changed mine."

Years later, I ran into another evangelist who had two conversations with Johan shortly before he was killed. God was chasing this man down in his incredible mercy.

Chapter 15: Reseed Chicago

Dave called to tell me that there was this preacher in Chicago who wanted to pass out gospel booklets all over the city, even the South Side. Dave said, "If you want to go, sign me up."

Dave and I caught the Amtrak train to Chicago. A bunch of people had volunteered, but, of the many thousands who promised to help with the distribution, only hundreds showed up. One big college, which was known for churning out stuck-up preachers, committed a thousand students to the effort. Not one showed up. The preacher got stuck with over a million pieces of leftover literature at a considerable expense for an inner-city church.

The preacher was an incredible guy, a lot like Dave. He just wanted to make sure heaven was full. His church had all kinds of different services such as Vietnamese and Sudanese, and they had about seventy people there for deaf services.

The group met the first evening, and the pastor said, "The Lord has laid it on my heart to go to the South Side."

I thought that if he was someone God was talking to, then I was on board. At that time, forty to fifty people a week were being shot on the South Side. We had only seven volunteers made up of four white guys, two black guys, and one Hispanic. They put Dave with the minorities and me with the two white preachers. We spent two days in the Englewood neighborhood.

I knew it was rough, but what I saw broke my heart, and in some ways healed my old wounds.

The first day we worked from nine to four. I jumped on the first porch full of young black men and shook hands with them. I didn't know if they were in a gang or not. I told them Jesus was the real deal. Around eleven o'clock some radio station wanted to interview the preachers I was with. I sat in the car watching teenagers walking by and thinking that tomorrow any one of these kids might be shot and go to hell.

I told the preachers that I was going on my own and wouldn't go further than the railroad tracks. I spoke with a nice Buddhist lady and a couple of older Christian men. They said they knew a seventeen-year-old kid who took some crack. He got so high that he didn't even remember shooting someone. One of the guys said, "Some of these kids won't listen to no one."

The two men exuded a deep sadness, and I sensed they had given up hope. Over the next two days, I saw many homes with bullet holes in them, and not one little kid looking out windows or out playing. I ran into a big gang down by the railroad tracks. They were shooting dice, looking at me like I was some kind of dinosaur. I gave a gospel booklet to the leader, but he wouldn't let me give out any more.

I couldn't help thinking that if they wanted to make some big money, they should buy some of these big brick homes. There was a house for $39,000, a big old stone-and-brick thing, which would go for over a million on the North Side if it were fixed up. They should buy up a bunch of these houses with their drug money, kick out the drug dealers, and they would all be permanently rich.

The gang leader wouldn't let me give my testimony, so I went to the next house, left a booklet there, and so on. They spread out like a wolf pack, but I wouldn't be intimidated. I had Jesus with me, after all. I just methodically dropped a booklet at every house.

I never realized it until later, but I had my "Got Jesus?" hat on. I don't really like that hat, but I had been working a lot and it was the only clean hat I had. Even though I couldn't talk with those gang members, they knew that Jesus sent a white man down their street because He loved their souls. That is why they looked at me like I was a dinosaur. They had never seen a lone white man there and probably never will again.

The Holy Spirit sets up incredible scenes like this. The closer you come to Jesus, the more you start to care about others. Scripture states that when you become a true believer, Jesus's Spirit enters you (John 3:6–8). It also says that without Jesus you can do nothing (John 15:5). So, the hat wasn't totally correct. The hat should have read, "Jesus Got Me."

It was the Jesus in me that saw those young gangsters and wanted to help them. That kind of love only comes from God. It wasn't that long ago when I was pounding those gangsters with my fists in my old neighborhood or pulling my knife out and threatening a whole carload of them back in the day.

Witnessing to others clearly wasn't me. It was Jesus in me. I was risking my life to save their souls. As we left that day, a cop who was a member of that church called to see if we were all right. Someone had just been shot after we left the neighborhood.

We spent another two days among the high rises in the wealthier part of Chicago. Dave and I probably handed out 5,000 booklets apiece. They had some big event going on downtown, and it was packed. There was a homeless, pregnant girl sitting on a corner next to a skinny old man. Her sign said, "Help. 19 years old. Two months pregnant and hungry." I talked with her for some time.

I noticed that the black folks were consistently more generous than the white ones, so I asked the girl if this was true. "It was always that way," she said. She figured that since they'd had more tough times, they were more sympathetic. I had seen the terrible conditions on the South Side, so it made sense to me.

There was an old man with a walker. He shook from the cold. I couldn't stand to watch any longer. No one had given him anything. I gave him twenty dollars and said, "Will you promise to spend it all on food?" He promised, but what he really did, who knows?

Half an hour later, the girl started shaking. I told her that she needed to go in the store behind us and warm up. She wouldn't because she didn't want to lose her spot. I told her I would hold the "I'm pregnant and hungry" sign and keep her spot for her. That gave her a good laugh, and I said, "Seriously, I'll make more money than you." But she wouldn't leave. Somebody bought her hot coffee and a sandwich. This girl looked so young, almost cowgirl wholesome. She just seemed so out of place with the rest of the homeless crowd.

I couldn't help thinking that her parents must be worried about her. "If you could have anything you wanted to get yourself out of here, what would it be?" I asked.

"A train ticket home to Fort Collins, Colorado. My boyfriend brought me here and took off. I'd just love to go home to my sister's place."

I asked her how much a ticket would cost, and she told me $235. I gave her my business card. "Tell you what. I'll be home in two days. I'll have somebody from the Baptist church purchase the ticket, but they're going to put you on the train. Jesus loves you. You call me in two days." She never did.

On my last day in Chicago, I was getting ready to get on the church bus to catch the train home when a small guy pulled up on a bike. I gave him a booklet. He glanced at it for a second and said, "You're a Christ lover. I've been practicing this German hymn for two years. Would you like to hear it?"

Leaning my good ear toward him, I told him yes. It was incredible, beautiful—unbelievably beautiful. I think he was an angel, the last person I spoke to on the streets of Chicago. These people in Chicago treated me like a prince and helped heal my "honky day" wounds, all while I was wearing my "Got Jesus?" hat.

Someone from Chicago told me that the black community still has an awe and respect for God and His people that doesn't exist in the wealthier parts of the city. That was my experience. There seemed to be a lot more good people than gangbangers.

After the Lord sent me back to the city, it struck a nerve with me about my heritage. I'm still an inner-city guy. I really love those kids, and I don't see that they have much hope. Why did only seven of the thousands that said they were going to take Jesus to the streets and the homes on the South Side show up? This is where they need the power of God the most.

A year and a half after I ran into Johan, my daughter and I were talking to two homeless drunks. They were sleeping in the snow under one blanket by the sewer heat vents near the college. They believed they were all right with Jesus. One of them said that he believed in Jesus. I explained that so did Satan. When you come to Jesus, He commands you to repent, which is to turn away from your sins. They didn't want to hear the truth, happy to sleep outside.

One of the drunks wanted to change the subject. He asked, "Hey, you ever met Johan? He's the number one drug dealer in Grand Rapids. He lives in a yellow house on Griggs Street."

I simply couldn't believe my ears. These guys knew the Muslim with the assassin angel tattoo. One guy said, "Yea, that guy's a crazy man. He's put a gun to my head twice."

I answered, "And I shared Jesus with him twice."

Chapter 16: Alaska Adventure

"Not everyone who says to Me, 'Lord, Lord,' shall enter the kingdom of heaven, but he who does the will of My Father in heaven" (Matthew 7:21). In 2013, I left my family and seasonal landscape business for twenty-five days because the Lord told me to. He instructed me to go to Alaska and tell others about Him. I had no formal church support, no reservations made for my journey, and I knew no one from Alaska.

Kelley and I sent letters to several churches, looking for a place to send our boxes of "Help From Above" (HFA) booklets, since carrying forty ten-pound boxes on a motorcycle was impossible. World Missionary Press told us they could send the boxes out there for us. All we needed was a place to ship them to, but numerous letters had come back as undeliverable, so I started contacting them by phone.

I reached a sweet-spirited woman named Cassie. She worked in the office at a Baptist church in Kenai. She said they would be glad to receive our literature and that there was a mission that I could probably work out of. She said she had received our letter, but we later realized we had never sent one; we didn't have their address. I guess the postal service performed a little miracle for us.

I left for Alaska on June 27, carrying what I could on my 1996, 500cc Kawasaki. Saying goodbye to my family brought tears to my eyes. Though Alaska was my destination, God had plans for my journey too.

In North Dakota, I marveled at how nature reveals the Godhead, shed tears for my unbelieving nation, and came up with my first country song. I gave out seven HFA booklets in Montana.

Canada seemed rich and clean, a beautiful country. It would be at least three days before I could bathe again in Haines, Alaska, so I washed my socks and underwear, drying them with the hotel hair dryer. I thought about the Lord, Kelley, and home.

The next day I ran into a storm and tried to sleep under my tarp. My back was sore. I smelled bad. But the sun came out, the birds were singing, and it was time to ride.

My back went out, but the Lord used it to give my testimony to three women from Yellowstone. There was a restaurant full of empty tables, and these women just sat down at my table as if we were old friends. I told them how Jesus cured my drinking problems. One of the women was a drug and alcohol counselor for some government agency. It was a God thing.

Next, I witnessed to Chris, the owner of a gas station. He said he didn't have time to talk. I offered him twenty dollars for his time if he would read an HFA booklet. He refused and said the New Testament made no sense. I left one in the window on the way out anyway and prayed that God would help him understand.

On July 4, it was twenty degrees and damp. I handed out four HFA booklets at the ferry office. The next day I rode 800 miles and gave out ten more.

Handing out HFA booklets as I went, I met a woman at a Baptist church that ran an outreach program. She was downright rude. For nine days, I'd found favor with most all the people I had met, but the first church leader I ran into blew me off.

After camping near a $189-a-night motel, I went to another Baptist church. I rode 5,000 miles to do street ministry, but the elders of the church wouldn't give me the time of day.

On July 8, I handed out two hundred HFA booklets at apartments and a boat launch. The next day, I started to stress out about logistics because I didn't see how I was going to hand out 20,000 HFA booklets without help. I met some guys painting a church and they took 400. The rehab director for the Salvation Army took 1,100 more. The Director for Youth Fishing Ministry took 2,500. I handed out about 700 at trailer parks and apartments. That's 4,700 in one day; not bad after a discouraging start.

Three days later, the Lord sent me to Soldotna, where I handed out five hundred booklets. I gave one to a nice kid named Jeremiah on the beach.

I met a guy from a local ministry on July 13. He wouldn't touch the 2,500 HFA booklets I offered them, even though he had a hundred kids working the beach, giving out hot dogs and water but not the Word of God. Then he asked me for money.

On July 16, the Lord told me I needed to love more and that my spirit was tired because I lacked love. I left 150 booklets at King Christian Bookstore. I then headed to Anchorage with 2,500 HFA booklets as soon as my bike was fixed.

The next day, we met Mr. English. He took two boxes of booklets to use in his Florida ministry. He said the Lord told him to give me $200. Wow, what a difference. A professional Christian wouldn't take my free literature and asked for money, while a volunteer missionary gave me money because God told him to. I overheard an older church lady saying I was stupid for bringing up 20,000 booklets. The 8,000 booklets left at the mission are not a testimony of my stupidity. They stand as a rebuke to one more spiritually dead church.

With my bike fixed, I headed out, dropping off HFA booklets as I went. Two hundred and fifty here, 550 there. A guy named Aaron told me to read Neil Cole's *Organic Church* book to understand why it seemed like the professional Christians were the only ones who had hindered my ministry on the whole trip. Aaron attended a small home church. I kept thinking God was going to do big things with little churches.

After breakfast on July 20, I left 350 booklets at a military base, and the Lord told me to pray more specifically for those people. He directed my paths, as He often does on campus ministry. He told me to go left down a street. I only had two booklets with me. There were two women sitting on a picnic table at the end of the street. I spoke to one of them for thirty minutes.

With one day left, I dropped off a box at Aaron's. He said it wouldn't be wasted. I wanted to hand out more, but the Lord wanted me to slow down. I went downtown and had a guy curse at me loudly. The Lord told me not to be a coward and go back. I asked Him to give me the right words to deal with this man who obviously hated Christians. We talked for about ten minutes and eventually shook hands. The Lord knows what words to use to get my attention.

On July 24, I sold my bike. The guy who bought it dropped me off at the airport. God's planning. On the plane, the Lord told me He wasn't altogether pleased with me for losing my temper with the folks who had hindered me. He told me that 310 lives would be positively affected by my twenty-five days in the north. God usually doesn't give me the results, but He knew I was discouraged. In nineteen years of street ministry, He's only told me the results three times.

Thank you, Lord, for using me to minister to others.

Of all the things I've learned through this, one of the best is that obedience to God's call is important. It seems like most of the big churches and large ministries are led by man's systems and not the Holy Spirit. The systems are a big machine, a heartless factory with no love. Too much busyness breaks fellowship with God and men, even if they are doing worthwhile things.

This frustrates me to no end, but God wants me to be more patient, show more love, and watch my anger closely (see Ephesians 4:26–27).

Soon after I returned home, my Baptist buddy criticized me, saying that God doesn't talk to people. However, John 10:27 says, "My sheep hear My voice, and I know them, and they follow Me"—like, to Alaska. Here are some other verses to consider; Matthew 21:22; John 9:31, 14:21; and Acts 5:32, 16:6, 20:22–23. Yes, indeed, where is the church that is spoken of in Acts?

This trip to Alaska cost me about $3,500. The Word says that God wishes to give us the desires of our hearts. Raising eight kids in Michigan, I couldn't have ever dreamed of this trip on my own. The Lord knows how I love the mountains He created. He had me put His Word in people's hands, and He blessed me with the best scenery in the world. Serving God is truly an adventure.

I encourage all my brothers and sisters in the Lord to set aside anything that seems more important than God. That's called idolatry. Set aside your pet sins because God won't hear your prayers (John 9:31). Ask Him to direct your paths where He could use you the most. Jesus surrendered His will to the Father. Surrender your will to the Father. He will bless you for it.

What I did for twenty-five days in Alaska will last forever, and I will see some of those people in heaven someday.

"I beseech you therefore, brethren, by the mercies of God, that you present your bodies a living sacrifice, holy, acceptable to God, which is your reasonable service. And do not be conformed to this world, but be transformed by the renewing of your mind, that you may prove what is that good and acceptable and perfect will of God" (Romans 12:1–2).

Chapter 17: Colorado Insights

The Holy Spirit directed me to write a new booklet. The ones that we had been using up until now had been great, but more of my street time was on college campuses now. We were doing less door-to-door stops.

I think the Lord wanted something more tailored to college students. Writing is difficult for me, and things just weren't coming together. One day the Lord told me, "Go to Montrose, Colorado."

I've been to Colorado, and it just didn't make sense to go again, so I asked God for confirmation. The next day at a restaurant there was a half-page article in *USA Today* about Montrose, Colorado. "Okay, Lord, you don't have to hit me over the head. I'll go."

My wife and I went. It was our first time doing street ministry together, and it was an ideal time for us to work on "us." Kelley had put up with a lot of nonsense over the years from me. With eight kids, we needed the time away. We worked four colleges and received a very tepid response. In fact, I left Colorado thinking that Satan had a better stranglehold on college campuses in that state than in Chicago. Some of the time we spent near Cortez in Montezuma County.

This was the inspiration for the new college booklet that I was to write, print, and hand out. I titled it *So, There Is No God*. Here is the text of that tract:

So, There Is No God

For the first thirty-one years of my life, I had believed this, even though I was brought up in a Christian home. After my Lyme disease had been misdiagnosed six times and I had lost twenty-five pounds from my already lean frame, I was in so much pain that I contemplated suicide. When you come face to face with death, you must finally face God or the concept of His existence.

I read the entire New Testament three times in three weeks. The Scriptures were interesting, but they didn't connect all the dots in my head. Scripture itself says that it is spiritually discerned, so you need the Spirit of God to help you fully understand it. I got some help from a wonderful Christian family that answered quite a few of my questions. At some point, I, in fact, believed, and that small amount of faith, through the power of the Holy Spirit, began to connect the dots. Amazingly, God answered my prayers, and some of them with incredible speed.

"For since the creation of the world His invisible attributes are clearly seen, being understood by the things that are made, even His eternal power and Godhead, so that they are without excuse, because, although they knew God, they did not glorify Him as God, nor were thankful, but became futile in their thoughts, and their foolish hearts were darkened. Professing to be wise, they became fools, and changed the glory of the incorruptible God into an image made like corruptible man—and birds and four-footed animals and creeping things . . . And even as they did not like to retain God in their knowledge, God gave them over to a debased mind, to do those things which are not fitting." (Romans 1:20–23, 28)

I had struggled to understand this because for thirty-one years I believed I had no knowledge of God. He has since shown me that I was so full of myself that there was no room for Him and His still small voice. I was an incredibly strong, funny, and fairly well-off, self-made man. God, in His mercy, used the destruction of my wealth and my body to break my pride. When your body is broken, and you're flat on your back, you have nowhere to look but up.

As a young Christian, I used to think that when God spoke of worshiping the creature and not the Creator, He was talking about golden calves and earth worshipers and such. The Scriptures clearly say that people worship created things rather than the Creator.

When a person is self-absorbed, he is in fact worshiping part of creation: himself. The typical American doesn't bow down to a golden calf. Rather, they worship themselves. These depraved people choose not to acknowledge God, so their minds become darkened.

When you have breakfast in just about any small-town restaurant, you'll hear the gray-haired folks often complaining about the end of morals, work ethics, common sense, and neighborliness. That's because the America of old was infused with the knowledge of God the Father and His Son, Jesus.

But knowledge of God has been attacked on every front: by the schools, the media, the government, the military, the churches, and the homes. According to the Scripture that we just read in Romans, when God knowledge is suppressed, depravity increases. Fifty years ago, nobody was getting shot in schools. Rapes and murders were almost unheard of. Nobody locked their doors, and nobody worried about their children being abducted.

So, let's look at another culture that was destroyed for lack of God knowledge. Many of the Indians of the woods and plains worshiped the Great Spirit. They didn't have the Word of God, but they realized they were created. But most of the Indians of the

Americas worshiped the creation and not the creator. The northern Indian tribes worshiped the bear, often calling him "Grandfather Bear." The more agrarian Indians worshiped the "Corn Mother." So now we have Mother Nature, Mother Earth, and so forth. Ancient pagans used much of the same language, symbols, thought patterns, and theories as our modern atheists or earth worshipers do today. Their shamans professed themselves to be wise and worshiped the things that God had created, and they became fools (Romans 1:22).

I once killed a bear in the Clearwater Mountains of Central Idaho, near the Lolo Trail, where the Lewis and Clark Expedition almost starved to death. When you skin a bear, minus the head, it resembles a well-muscled man.

For hundreds, and maybe even thousands, of years, we have the Indians worshiping the bear that had a similar build. Now we have Darwin and his monkey. But there is no physical proof that man evolved from apes.

Darwin's daughter died at an early age, so in his anger Darwin rejected God. He got the answers that his darkened and selfish heart wanted—a world without God.

I have spent a great deal of time trying to show that rejecting God is everyone's way of being not accountable, and we all do it, even far too many people in the church. Please don't judge God by the people who claim to be His.

I once tried to counsel a young man who was struggling in his faith. I told him that in China, if you claim faith in Christ, you will most certainly lose your government job and possibly your home. Yet, the church is growing like crazy, approaching a hundred million. I asked what would happen if the people in his church would have to pay that price for Jesus. He said the church would be empty.

Remember that Jesus died for your sins. It's a personal decision you must make. Your relationship with God is your responsibility. Running into some false Christians doesn't excuse you for your sins. The Scriptures say that in the last days there will be a falling away. Many churches have already left God and truth, but they're still there every weekend for their social hour.

Many Christians believe that the USA is ripe for destruction. Look how God judged Israel under King Manasseh (2 Kings 21:6–14) for sacrificing their children to false gods. God destroyed the North American Indians because they worshiped the creation, not the Creator. God used Cortez and European diseases to wipe out the Aztecs for the same dark-minded behavior of Manasseh's kingdom.

Ask the God of the universe to guide you into all truth. Don't you absolutely hate it when you find out someone has lied to you? The typical American has embraced countless lies. Let me show you a few.

Modern-day scholars believe that Jesus was born in June, so why do we celebrate Christmas in December? We also decorate the Christmas tree, an allegedly Christian symbol. Yet, this was a pagan earth worship symbol, probably Germanic in origin. Modern-day Robin Hoods steal from the rich and give to the poor—good socialists. The real Robin Hood stole from the tax collectors, and he gave the money back to the people who were taxed. Two popular, state-sponsored lies are that there are no moral absolutes and that man evolved from apes.

The Aztec sun god's name was Huitzilopochtli, and he was depicted as a snake, like the biblical serpent, Satan. Even though there is no evidence that the Aztecs had the Scriptures, they still knew Satan's name. Is this an incredible coincidence, or is it evidence that Satan speaks to his people also?

Visualize a captured Indian held by his arms and legs by four men while an Aztec priest cuts out his heart and throws it on a burning altar to their sun god. The sacrificed man, who was given nothing to ease the pain, is tossed down the stairs of the temple. This is gruesome but historically true. Everyone knows what happened to the Aztecs.

"He who sacrifices to any god, except to the Lord only, he shall be utterly destroyed" (Exodus 22:20). The Aztecs were destroyed because God hated their deeds. Proverbs 6:16–17 shows us that God hates those who shed innocent blood. The Aztecs sacrificed many thousands of innocents to their sun god.

Americans have sacrificed many millions of innocent children to their self-god. You see, God must destroy America, but you have been given this warning so you can repent. God destroyed my wealth and body so that I would seek the truth. As you witness God destroying America, you also may—unless you're destroyed first—have an opportunity to repent for your selfishness.

Let's fast forward to the present to a good-looking feminist that can't bear the thought of having to raise another unwanted child. Raising two alone is already enough. She has held onto this child for twenty-eight weeks, believing that the baby might entice her fourth live-in boyfriend to stay, but last weekend he disappeared. She knows that she must go to the abortion clinic, immediately. The doctor straps her to the chair, removes her young child with his sharp knives, giving the child nothing for the pain. Her pro-choice priest throws the butchered child in the trash, where it will be incinerated later in the day.

Look at the horrible price that her unborn child has paid because the adults around this child have embraced demonic practices that have been inspired by Satan in the hearts of men. Hearts that have been darkened because they have chosen not to acknowledge God and His law that He has written on every man's heart.

It is scary to see how similar the practices of the Aztecs are to modern-day abortionists. When Satan takes over someone's thinking, it almost always ends in death, and often eternal death. The Scripture says that Satan loves death. You must understand that Satan was God's most powerful angel. He wanted to be like God. He wanted to be worshiped and make his own rules. He loves it when people mindlessly follow him, giving their blood sacrifices to him, and, in the process, pay the price of eternal fire for the shedding of innocent blood.

For over six thousand years, his demons have taught the depraved how to murder in a way that Satan enjoys. Look at the differences. God dies for us, shedding Jesus's blood, while Satan kills us any which way he can. God's followers live with Him in a paradise of eternal joy, while Satan and his followers dwell in the realm of eternal death.

The true God created life and loves life, but He will not force you to take it. He gets glory when people willingly acknowledge Him and praise His Son.

We've left future generations with a morally and financially bankrupt nation. Our children will be slaving away their entire lives to pay for the bills of a crooked government. Can you see how God is cursing our newly paganized culture and blessing an up-and-coming Chinese Christian culture?

Just like Cortez destroyed the Aztec's military with the force of a thousand men, America faces a militant Russia and China. If history repeats itself, Russia or China could easily defeat an arrogant, pagan America, or maybe God will use the coronavirus to punish us. Some historians believe that as many as twenty-five million Aztecs were killed by the diseases brought by Cortez's men. Who will be America's Cortez?

You see that the word "pro-choice" has a much deeper spiritual meaning. This is a word that the enemies of God have chosen to describe themselves. As I have shown, the book of Romans is clear. They have chosen not to acknowledge the God that created the universe, created all life, and crowned our lives as His supreme creation. Please, call on Jesus with an honest and humble heart.

It is my sincere hope that you will see through the lies that this culture has dumped on you. It will be with incredible joy that I hope to see you hanging out with Jesus someday on the other side.

Freedom is not just the right to choose. But true freedom is found in making the right choices. His name is Jesus.

Chapter 18: Tearing Down the House

On the way home from Colorado, we met up with an old friend in Lincoln, Nebraska. He said he had had a dream of our children running around our yard with a big mean black dog. He thought the dog represented the devil. His dream would soon turn into our worst nightmare.

I worked eight months out of the year as a landscape contractor. The economy had been lean in Michigan since 2007, so I scaled my company back to one crew, which put me in the loader most of the time. Lyme disease had damaged my joints, and it was the worst thing for me to do, but it was the only thing I'd done for thirty-five years, and I had to provide for my family. I was under an incredible amount of stress. I didn't know it at the time, but my Lyme disease had come back.

We'd worked with another contractor for ten years or so. He had built some stone walls for us and some decks. This contractor, I would eventually discover, was one of the crookedest conmen in the area. But I learned this only after he cost me $15,000.

He had ripped off dozens of people we would run into later. This guy was a very accomplished purveyor of poop. He was just biding his time and completing small jobs for me so that he could rip me off on a big project. The stress of dealing with him and the pain of my recurrent Lyme disease made me unbearable to work with. At the time, one of my teenage daughters was working with me. She'd always been rebellious, but these events had the effect of putting a wedge between us.

This contractor had lied to me so many times that I finally lost it. I wasn't the kind of guy to "go postal" on someone, so I brought a selection of knives and clubs over to a jobsite that I knew he would be working at.

The intention was to have a modern-day duel. This guy outweighed me by about seventy-five pounds, but I knew what the outcome would be. It was my intention to make the world a better place. With him six feet under, it would have been. When I got to the jobsite, the place was crawling with other people.

He had an employee who I felt would tell the truth—that I had given this guy his choice of weapons and had a fair and honorable fight. But, with all these other people around, I wasn't so sure I would get a fair trial after I killed this crook, so I left. Once again, God protected me from my anger.

My anger and bitterness had taken me far from God. I'm glad that all those people were there because I probably would have killed him that day. The Bible tells us that vengeance is the Lord's (Deuteronomy 32:35) and that we are supposed to love and pray for our enemies (Matthew 5:44). Now I pray for this guy, that God will help him change like He helped me.

This perfect storm thoroughly wrecked my relationship with my daughter. It breaks my heart that I wasn't there for her in her later teenage years when she really needed me. I realize I had believed a lie for a long time: that my temper, which had helped me survive in the ghetto, was somehow a tool that I could use to get my work done faster and solve my problems.

However, it caused my daughter and me to have an incredible blowup. A year or so later, she turned her back on me. The distinct possibility that I may have forever lost a most special child still hangs over my head. Now my temper is, for the most part, dead, and it will only be used to save someone else's life or soul, if I can help it. There is such a thing as righteous anger, but it is an easy line to cross.

That winter, the pain of the Lyme disease was incredible, worse than my first bout. The headaches and joint pain were unbearable. My stomach had been severely damaged from medications from a back injury, so I couldn't find an oral painkiller that wouldn't make my insides bleed.

I reached a point where I just wanted to die. I even spoke to the Lord one day about taking Bibles into Somalia or some other dangerous mission that He could put me on. I knew that suicide was a sin, and the last thing in my life was not going to be sin. I'd done plenty of that already. Then the Holy Spirit said, "Scott, you're going to die this week."

I was relieved and wrote up my will. Later in the week, I took the kids out to my favorite piece of woods to do some winter camping. Two of my buddies showed up at my winter camp, and I thought, *Thanks, Lord, for the send-off.* My week was up, and I would soon be dead.

While asking the Lord why, He put a Scripture in my mind: "Or do you not know that your body is the temple of the Holy Spirit who is in you, whom you have from God, and you are not your own? For you were bought at a price" (1 Corinthians 6:19–20). The Lord was teaching me that my life was His—all of it. He was going to take me when He wanted to. He owns my life to use as He pleases.

That's what He meant by saying that I would die that week. The old me, the old selfish me, needed to be put to death.

God expected me to give Him everything in my life that was more important than Him. Then I realized that my twenty acres in the Idaho mountains, where I had dreamed of a log cabin with a stone fireplace, were too important to me. I offered it up for sale and was going to give the money to the World Missionary Press. There had been three guys who were really interested in buying it, but now nobody had any money. I had passed the test. The Lord didn't want that property, He just wanted true obedience. My Lyme disease went away.

Anything that is more important than God is *your* god. The Lord wants every piece our hearts. He doesn't want to take second place to anything. If you're truly His child, He will take away anyone or anything that is more important to you than He is—or at least lower its value in your eyes. In one week, He had totally devalued one of my lifelong dreams, a trapper's cabin in the mountains.

Now He was going to teach me charity His way.

We do Bible studies daily with our children in the wintertime. We started a study on the orphans in Uganda. We read *Kisses from Katie* and watched a few movies. When we finished the study, I told the kids that we should pray that the Lord would lead us in the proper direction and that the Holy Spirit would show us the right place to help.

While I prayed, the Lord told me twenty, just the number twenty.

One of the leaders of our church had a son who had started a school in Uganda. I wasn't thinking the school would necessarily be what God wanted us to do. So I just casually asked them how many orphans still needed sponsors. You guessed it, twenty.

Years previously, we had given a generous sum of money to a missionary we liked, but his local agent stole our donation along with other people's. This was when I was a new Christian and didn't understand how the Lord directs those who are obedient to His will.

Now, if I must make a major decision, I won't act unless the Lord makes it clear that I should. We do this even when we buy a car. If I had just been following Jesus instead of men or my own plans, I would never have given any money to that crook.

The Holy Spirit told me to write this book. I think it's because so many people are following spiritual leaders they shouldn't be following.

The gospel is simple. You recognize you're a sinner who needs to be released from your sins. You accept the gift of salvation from Jesus, and you pick up your cross and follow Him.

Over time, you develop a close relationship with Jesus, who takes your character defects and uses them as tools to teach you and others to live in a way that pleases God. Then He gives you certain gifts that make you more effective. If you're obedient, He directs you daily to walk in the path that He has made for you so that you might have treasure in heaven.

Jesus will have billions of adoring fans in heaven, and I'm His adopted brother whom He has taught His Father's business, which is saving those people from hell who are truly searching for the truth. So then, in eternity, I'll have many best friends in heaven whom I will have helped find Jesus.

Jesus is our example. He submitted to a horrible death on the cross for His Father and for us. The death that I must submit to is the death of my will. My desires of a cabin in the mountains are over. My dream now is to be even closer to Jesus so that I can witness even bigger miracles on the streets of America. He has given me a new, better dream.

I bought a new bicycle for my boy at Walmart. As he pushed it through the store, there must have been a dozen people who smiled at him, sharing in his joy. As I got to the cash register, I was tearing up, and I said, "Lord, these are my people. I love them. Please help them find your Son."

We all need Him. Think about people in history and the decisions they made. Do you think Joseph Stalin had any connection whatsoever to God? How about Hitler? How about the hundreds of pedophile priests? I get angry just thinking about it and want to put someone's head through a wall. The old me still flares up at times.

———

The Lord told me to take $5,000 for another mission trip to Alaska. I tried to take another $1,000, but He rebuked me. We were gone for twenty-one days, and we had just enough. The Lord sent the whole family to Alaska. What a journey.

The Holy Spirit had told me to go to Talkeetna. Before we got there, we distributed about 3,000 Scripture booklets in the Anchorage area. We then handed out booklets along the Kenai River when the red salmon began to run in July.

We met a young man at the Soldotna Museum, and we had instant fellowship, like Chris at the trailer park. When we saw him again in Homer, about a hundred and fifty miles away, he told us about his plans for a camp for troubled youth. I made informal arrangements to buy a parcel of land from him on the spot. I had just met the man, but I felt it was God's will to someday help him out there.

We traveled to Talkeetna. We had no reservations and just let God plan the trip as we went. As we approached Talkeetna, it was close to six o'clock. We stopped at a church that was having a Bible study, and the Lord wanted us to stay there.

There were twenty-five people at the church. The pastor said that sometimes he struggled when he felt the Lord leading him to share his faith. Then, he turns on a movie on evangelism. We had just shared the gospel with thousands of people. Guess who taught the class that night?

We then stayed at an elder's home. They owned a huge yak ranch with beautiful huge dogs that he said protected the animals from the grizzlies. The kids had a blast feeding the animals. It brought tears to my eyes. What are the chances that the Lord would tell me to go to Talkeetna two years before this and that we would reach this destination at the perfect time?

Here's another amazing thing about the trip. Our truck had been running on seven cylinders since the Yukon, so I changed out one of the cylinder plugs. The check engine light went off, and it ran much better. We had scheduled a mechanic two days out to fix it, and we were planning on staying longer to have a professional look at it. That cylinder ran well for the last time on the way out. The check engine light came back on again by Anchorage, and, on our way back home, the vehicle was running on seven cylinders again. We drove that old Expedition all the way back to Michigan on seven cylinders.

We took the kids and some of our friends to Michigan State University in the fall to hand out booklets. We had a friend, John, praying that other Christians would show up and help us. When we arrived, we had many Christian students join us.

Some of them requested prayer because they were struggling with the worldliness of the campus, and others just cheered us on. It was one of our best days on campus. One young man had incredible energy and was full of joy and the Holy Spirit. He must have handed out two hundred booklets.

I knew that John's prayers paved the way for our success that day. It was the single biggest day we'd ever had, and almost 6,000 students received the truth. That Friday night, we were driving home from a church function, and I was telling the kids how incredible it was to see God pouring out His Holy Spirit.

I commented how I wished I had my money stolen from me so that I could be on the streets all the time. Just as I said this, a huge shooting star flashed in front of our vehicle for all to see, as if God himself was giving us a sign. I knew it came from Him, but I didn't know for what. At first, I thought *He might be giving me the funds for full-time ministry.*

I tossed and turned until two o'clock in the morning.

At various times over the years, the Lord had directed my hands to open the Bible to the exact page I needed to read. This morning, I opened my Bible to Revelation 9, part of John's vision of the end of this era. I believe the Lord wanted to show me that we are in the last days and He is pouring out His Holy Spirit.

Sometime in the spring, the Holy Spirit told me that landscaping was again taking too much out of me. The Lord told me to take eleven gospel booklets and turn left out of my drive. This is unusual as I normally carry a whole box. He directed me to an old friend's house. I gave the eleven booklets to my buddy's daughter. I didn't understand it. I told her I was embarrassed, but the Lord told me to do it, and I had no idea why. Next, He sent me to a small town with one large church. As I drove by, the Lord said, "There is no life (Holy Spirit) there."

Then He sent me to a friend's business and told me to pray for her. I started to get out and go to see her, but the Lord said, "No, just pray." Next, He sent me to another friend's house, someone we used to fellowship with whose wife had died. He had been drinking heavily ever since she passed. He was happy to see me at 10:00 a.m. with a beer in hand. He wanted to show me something on the internet.

As I went in, I silently prayed, "Lord, give me the right words to help him quit."

I asked him, "How many practicing homosexuals will there be in heaven?"

"None," he said with a smile.

"How many practicing drunks? What's Scripture say in Galatians 5:19–21?"

He then started on a rant about how his wife died.

I told him that was a long time ago.

Then the Lord sent me to a house at the end of a cul-de-sac close to my buddy's and told me to pray against the demons that were in that house. This is something that I had never done.

The last stop that day was at what I thought was an empty auditorium. The Lord was clearly telling me to go left, and I told him the place was empty. Just then, I noticed an older gentleman working on something in the basement. Tapping on the door, I gave him my only booklet. The Lord knew this was a guy who wanted the truth.

I was home for lunch.

One of the elders of the church we were going to at that time had relatives there, and I warned them about the leadership being most likely false. Months later, I learned that the church God had told me had no life had just come under new leadership.

My old friend that I gave eleven tracks to was leaving the state and leaving two daughters and their husbands and seven grandchildren behind. Hence the eleven gospel tracts I had left with his daughter. These children were going to the same type of spiritually dead church I went to as a child.

As you read all the street ministry miracles, it's important to note that nothing of eternal importance is constructed outside the power of the Holy Spirit. There is simply no credit or glory that goes to me. The miracles I've seen on the streets were all executed by Jesus. Jesus receives all the glory for it's His work. I'm just along for the ride.

Chapter 19: College Ministry

One spring the Lord told me to go to a nearby college. The police had kicked me off campus a few years earlier, so I thought *we ought to bring a camera just in case things get crazy.* As soon as we got there, the cops were on us, asking us for our IDs, which is unconstitutional. There was no probable cause of a crime being committed. I called their bluff and told them that if they arrested me, I would sue them for violating my free speech rights. This day was one of the most powerful examples in my life about how the Holy Spirit works.

As we drove in, a huge blue and white sign read, "Special Event Today." Unknown to us, the public high schools were visiting that day. As these students left the busses, they just assumed we were part of the special event, and every student took a booklet. We handed out between 350 to 400 booklets.

The Lord told me that thirty-four students began their special relationship with Jesus, just as I had done some twenty years earlier. God was chasing down people who were searching for the truth. The Lord used my family and a friend to deliver thirty-four curious people to an eternity with God despite all efforts of Satan's public institutions in America and their war against Christ.

Most interesting of all, it had nothing to do with the bricks and mortar that people call church. Just one man led by the Holy Spirit with Jesus again as our example.

In Matthew Jesus tells us to pick up our cross and follow Him (Matthew 16:24).

In John He says, "My sheep hear My voice, and I know them, and they follow Me. And I give them eternal life, and they shall never perish; neither shall anyone snatch them out of My hand" (John 10:27–28).

Later Paul writes: "For as many as are led by the Spirit of God, these are sons of God" (Romans 8:14).

Finally, we read, "In all your ways acknowledge Him, and He shall direct your paths" (Proverbs 3:6).

One of my first memories of the works of the Holy Spirit occurred soon after I became a believer. My daughters were singing at a church, and my father had come to hear them. When the preacher—my friend Dave—started his message, he got flustered. "I . . . was going to preach about Daniel, but the Lord wants me to preach about Moses." As the minister went through the story of Moses, he kept repeating "forty years." Moses ran from God and spent forty years in the desert. During the sermon, my father was tearing up. When the service was over, he hurried out to his car just after promising me that someday he would tell me about "forty years."

Later, he shared that it was forty years since he was at Hope College studying to be a preacher when he left college to start his own business. He believed in Jesus but had never had the spiritual birth. God used this minister's message about Moses and forty years to draw my father into a serious commitment to and relationship with Jesus, which would occur about one year later.

Another time, my oldest boy and I were at a restaurant, and there was a middle-aged woman crying nonstop. I couldn't stand it. I asked her if there was anything I could do to help. She had six kids and had just lost her job. I asked her about her immediate bills. I offered her $500 and told her that my wife and I would sit down with her on Saturday and see if we could help her find another job and get her life in order.

My intention was to help her out and share what Jesus had done in my life with her. The weekend ended, and we had heard nothing from her. That Wednesday, a contractor friend of mine came up to me and said, "You know that girl with the tattoo on her neck? She died of a drug overdose Friday night." She hadn't called me because Satan had beaten me to her soul. I always have some kind of gospel booklet with me. I should have told her about Jesus. I just thought there would be time for that later. Tricked by the father of all lies, again.

Two months before writing this book, I was still struggling to figure out why my street ministry had been more powerful and productive when I wasn't attending church for two years. Writing down my story has helped me to clarify my thoughts on many things. I know that I haven't arrived, and I don't suppose that anyone can know all of God's truth. I have only seen a small part of our great and loving Creator. He has already rewarded me greatly. Please Lord, help me submit everything I do and say to your plan.

The day that I met the woman who later overdosed, I was in a really good mood, happy to be out there with my boy, content with my own plans for the day, and not surrendered or led by the Holy Spirit. How did I hatch this plan in my head to help her with her finances, like I'm some government agency or something? Pray for her kids, would you?

At this time, I believe that we are preparing to leave the brick-and-mortar church for good. All the major dreams of my life will hopefully be made by the Holy Spirit. God sees me just like I see a little child. Jesus has the whole picture, and I only see bits and pieces. I will defer my life to His better judgment.

Now, don't go out and shoot the preacher—like I wanted to as a kid—because he is just like all of us, just another sinner. But be careful who you follow. If his life and philosophy doesn't square up with the Bible, then run.

While finishing the first draft of this story, I approached an older black man from Texas in a restaurant. The Lord even warned me that it wasn't going to go well. As we talked about racism, the gentleman claimed that President Obama had improved race relations dramatically. The man claimed he was personally color-blind.

I told him that, when I was a young kid, I was beaten up by blacks many times because of my color. He wouldn't believe it and quickly told me to go. My experience didn't fit his worldview. He had not one ounce of empathy for me. The man wasn't color-blind. His color completely defined his worldview.

When I told him about the beatings, he said that it must have been the other way around—seven or eight white teenagers beating a little black kid. He implied that I was lying and that I had twisted the players around.

Not once have I discounted a black man's story about racism, but what would compel this one to immediately discount mine? I have concluded that Satan's influence of bitterness often makes people become what they hate. In fact, the worst racists I've ever known were black. The blacks have a much deeper, longer historical timeline of abuse than any inner-city white kid could claim, but the bitterness on both sides is simply not productive. This cannot solve the problem. Somehow racism must be reduced to its most damaging symptom, which is bitterness. Bitterness destroys the person who carries it. Therefore, you must forgive to live.

The question is, how do we move forward? How can we prevent a race war and our cities from burning?

As you know by now, Jesus has all the answers. He commands us to love our neighbors as ourselves. Treat them the way you want to be treated. Listen to their stories.

We all have pain, but we must learn to forgive. The goodness of the people in Chicago helped to heal my heart from the "honky day" crowd. I think ninety percent of all people, regardless of color, are decent folks. So why are we allowing the minority of the population that really are racist to define what it really is and beat us over the head with their bitterness?

I've watched Martin Luther King speeches and seen his picture often. His face does not exude bitterness like some other well-known speakers. How have these bitter people become spokesmen for the black community? We are not going to solve racism with greater racism from the other side.

Only the embodiment of Jesus's love will turn this around. We must learn to mingle and to love each other, or we are in big trouble. Every human has good qualities because we've been created in God's image. You can find beauty and nastiness in all people. The trait you choose to focus on is the one you will get.

Chapter 20: A Bad Day

After fasting three days, the Holy Spirit told me to drive north. He said I was going to have a bad day. I found myself in my old neighborhood. I spoke with a rough-looking couple, telling them how Jesus had changed me. The Lord sent me to the church I went to when I was a kid and told me to go in. I so didn't want to, but I did. As I walked through the church, I saw the balcony where we used to sit. I started to cry. It was like it tore my guts out. All these years had gone by, and just the sight of it brought back my old pain.

One of the staff noticed my odd behavior and asked if he could help me. Between tears, I told him I was going through bad memories.

Walking back to the van, the Holy Spirit told me to tell the preacher why. I headed back to the church. The staff stood on the sidewalk watching me. I asked to speak with the preacher. The pastor seemed like a nice fellow. I told him that some folks at that church treated me like shit when I was a kid, and that the experience almost sent me to hell.

The emotions kept pouring over me all afternoon, leaving me useless for the rest of the day. I had no idea my pain ran so deeply. I headed over to my sister's house to talk about this with her before I made the forty-five-minute drive home. She told me that I needed to forgive them.

I got home and shared this with my wife. She also told me that I needed to forgive them. Then she revealed another layer to the onion I'd been peeling back. She asked if I could imagine how my mom must have felt. "This wasn't your sin or her sin. It was your dad's sin for leaving her high and dry in the hood with eight kids."

The truth just screams at you, doesn't it? It seems like there's an awful lot of people in this world suffering because of other people's sins. In their rage, they sin. It's like a gerbil running in a wheel. Sin begets more sin.

Look at most of these gangbangers in Chicago—little or no contact with a loving father—just like me.

Millions of kids are left high and dry in the hood. Someone told me that ninety-three percent of the kids on the south side of Chicago have no father contact. Our relationships with our earthly fathers should mirror those of our Heavenly Father. But with no dads in their homes, they have no Heavenly Father to trust or fellowship with. The fruit of which is two hundred shootings a month. The Bible says that in the last days there would be continual violence. This explains the rage in their hearts.

When my finances collapsed and my Lyme disease came back, my rage destroyed my relationship with one of my daughters. Do you know what? She left God too. Can you see Satan's hand on my family, and his death grip on the hood? Destroy the family unit that God established, damaging and destroying most of those outside of it, and you have a lost and raging society.

I wrote this chapter two years after the rest of this book. My statements about racial pain may seem a little bit flippant, implying that somehow you can just turn off the hurt. Well, the Lord showed me that we all try to sweep the pain under the rug. In the process, we don't see what has been tearing us up inside.

We have all these hurts piled up inside, and Jesus wants them gone. He wants us to forgive. It simply never crossed my mind that I must forgive those nasty old ladies at church with their noses held so high.

There are millions of Americans who will never set foot in a church due to thoughtless people and wicked leadership. But the truth is that you don't have to set foot in a church. Just walk straight into the arms of Jesus. He's the real deal. Jesus loved this crazy old man when I was totally unlovable.

Jesus will never stick His nose up at you or roll His eyes. Look at who Jesus hung out with when He walked the Earth: stinky fishermen, tax collectors, and prostitutes.

I beg you to open your eyes to this same Jesus. He's waiting with His arms open wide. He wants fellowship with you, whoever you are and wherever you might be.

The Big Picture

This book is about my relationship with God. Though I don't deserve it, my Heavenly Father protected me (and continues to do so) during the raucous and rebellious phase of my life. Then Jesus saved me. Now the Holy Spirit directs me as I seek to serve God and tell others the good news of Jesus.

But this book is also about my relationship with the church. And it's a strained one, with the institution of church doing me more harm than good, thwarting my efforts at evangelism and obeying God's call.

It's been my experience that the so-called church lacks the power of God, in part because the leadership has embraced the business model instead of the Holy Spirit. They let man's plans supersede God's. "[They have] a form of godliness but denying its power. And from such people turn away!" (2 Timothy 3:5).

Until I stepped away from the four walls that folks call church, I saw very few miracles. Since then, I have never run into a church leader who has seen anywhere near the number of miracles I have.

The logical conclusion I've come to is that God's power resides more outside of organized religion than in it. I've often visualized Jesus coming into the church and tipping over the money changer tables. But Jesus hasn't done this. He left the building and took His power with Him.

Consider a small town near where we used to live. On one side of the road sits a small old brick church. Across the street stands a large modern church.

On Easter Sunday the small brick church sign read, "He is risen."

The larger flashing church sign across the road read, "1000s of Easter eggs."

One church spoke of the power of God and the other marketed entertainment to boost their numbers, I assume. I'd rather walk in the power of the Holy Spirit by myself and not into a large church full of entertainment-minded Christians marketing Jesus.

In another instance, one of our friends had a flat tire in the parking lot of a mega church. Everyone left the service without offering to help. This stranded family, with three young kids, watched these self-centered, so-called believers pass them by without even a word of assistance.

I like to tell people who claim to be Christians that Satan believes in Jesus too. So what makes them different from Satan? I think Satan would ignore this young family and leave them to suffer on Sunday.

Is it any wonder that Americans reject the church and then reject God's Son and the incredible future only He can offer?

The leaders of most every denomination bemoan the loss of members and the waning influence of the church. But the foundation of most of their ministries is in direct opposition to the words that Jesus spoke: "Heal the sick, cleanse the lepers, raise the dead, cast out demons. Freely you have received, freely give" (Matthew 10:8).

If you get off to a false start, you inevitably end up with a business model church. (That's why, whenever possible, I give away this e-book for free and offer the paperback at cost.) Paul said that he worked with his hands so as not to damage the cause of Christ (see Acts 18:3 and 2 Corinthians 11:7).

But church leadership fails to see that their model was broken from the start. They blame the decline of the church on Satan, while each day they defy God's words. Yes, I suppose they are right; it is the work of Satan in their hearts and their minds. Because of this, the church in the United States is damaged and on life support.

We need to call on Jesus to raise up more volunteers and make a bunch of professionals either repent or retire.

If you wish to see the power of God, walk away from man's systems, and watch God work like you've never seen before. Just make sure you make your life completely compliant with God's Word and the direction of the Holy Spirit. God's eyes still search the earth for those completely sold out to Him and His work (see 2 Chronicles 16:9).

Jesus warned the church that unless they repented, He would remove their lampstand (see Revelation 2:5). This is His light and power, which, as I have shown you, is mostly missing from the so-called churches I've attended in the last twenty-five years.

I'm hopeful that you can find a little church that really looks and acts like the early church, full of love and humble leadership. If you find it, hang on tight, and send me a note. Before I die, I'd like to see a church function like it's written in the book of Acts.

The initial title of this book was *Shoot the Preacher*. As you may recall in chapter 1, when I was five years old, that's what I considered doing: shoot the preacher—with my BB gun. Figuratively, I still feel like that. But that title would never be approved in the oversensitive, politically correct mindset that pervades the United States today.

But the metaphor of "shoot the preacher" is a recurring theme in this book. I say this because I think most believers would be better off without their current leaders.

I encourage you to examine yourselves and the church leadership you're under to see how well they minister based on the red letters in the Bible and the book of Acts. Look at what Jesus said.

Ask yourself if your church lives out Jesus's words and not man's philosophies. Search for God with all your heart. His words are true. Believe them and live.

You won't regret it.

Key Verses in the Bible

Do not be deceived, God is not mocked; for whatever a man sows, that he will also reap (Galatians 6:7).

But your iniquities have separated you from your God (Isaiah 59:2).

For all have sinned and fall short of the glory of God (Romans 3:23).

He who covers his sins will not prosper, but whoever confesses and forsakes them will have mercy (Proverbs 28:13).

Wash yourselves, make yourselves clean; put away the evil of your doings from before My eyes. Cease to do evil (Isaiah 1:16).

For Christ also suffered once for sins, the just for the unjust, that He might bring us to God (1 Peter 3:18).

Nor is there salvation in any other, for there is no other name under heaven given among men by which we must be saved (Acts 4:12).

Repent therefore and be converted, that your sins may be blotted out (Acts 3:19).

"Come now, and let us reason together," says the Lord, "Though your sins are like scarlet, they shall be as white as snow; though they are red like crimson, they shall be as wool" (Isaiah 1:18).

For by grace you have been saved through faith, and that not of yourselves; it is the gift of God, not of works, lest anyone should boast (Ephesians 2:8–9).

If we confess our sins, He is faithful and just to forgive us our sins and to cleanse us from all unrighteousness (1 John 1:9).

He who has the Son has life; he who does not have the Son of God does not have life (1 John 5:12).

But as many as received Him, to them He gave the right to become children of God, to those who believe in His name (John 1:12).

For as many as are led by the Spirit of God, these are sons of God (Romans 8:14).

The greatest miracle of all is that God wants fellowship with each of us. Only at the name of His Son does He open that door. -Scott Bartleson

About the Author

Raised by a godly, single mother, Scott Bartleson suffered ridicule and rejection at the church they attended. This forever strained his relationship with church and damaged his view of God, sending Scott on a wild rampage.

Then God got Scott's attention, and under Holy Spirit power, he became God's wild man.

This former miscreant followed God's direction and began to tell others about Jesus. Many times, his work took a back seat to witnessing. God used Scott to change people's lives, bring them into relationship with him, and point them to eternity.

Scott expects to see many of the people he met on his wild adventures waiting for him when he arrives in heaven. What a glorious reunion that will be.